Alone in
Arabian Nights

Alone in
Arabian Nights

by

SIRDAR IKBAL ALI SHAH

THE OCTAGON PRESS
LONDON

ISBN 0 863040 63 2

First published 1933
Introduction first published for 2nd edition 1939
Revised by Author in 1969
First published in this edition 1992

Photoset, printed and bound by
Redwood Press, Melksham, Wiltshire

Contents

Introduction

Professor Sir Edward Denison Ross, Kt.,
CIE., D.Litt., PhD.

This is one of the most extraordinary books I have ever read: both because of its erudition, scope and range, and because its Author – well known to me for many years – is so tremendously modest about his achievements.

It is perhaps less unusual in the East than in the West for someone with illustrious and ancient titles, with an imperial and holy lineage, to be found tackling highwaymen and learning how to sell trinkets. Even so, I can say, as an Orientalist myself, that it is not as common as all that.

The Sirdar Ikbal Ali, Shah, possesses, as of right, the style of Badshah (King), of His Sublime Highness, and a score of other honorifics. This does not stop him lodging in caravanserais, living like a penniless dervish and, if I may say so, writing the most excellently idiomatic English.

So you will see that this most fascinating of books really needs no introduction at all, as those long-winded worthies always say when winding up the usual redundant disquisition until the after-dinner speaker does his stuff.

So here you are: the treat of a lifetime, from the greatest contemporary writer and traveller of the East!

Edward Denison Ross
Tehran

1

To the Holy Shrines

Ask what beauty is, and you will receive – of course – indefinite and varying replies. It is so because you cannot describe beauty. So, too, it is with travel.

You cannot describe the feeling of enjoyment which arises in the mind when you travel: the sensation of wondrous exhilaration upon beholding the melting of colours over mountaintops on a new-born day: Or the feeling into which the mind plunges on seeing an old and battered castle on the edge of a sleeping desert, emerging as it does through the mists of an enchanted past.

The motives of a real log-roller or the overnighter in many a caravanserai is as difficult to give in matter-of-fact words as the explanation of any of those feelings.

This, in essence, is the philosophy of a globetrotter. Not that he or she travels in order to arrive at any particular destination. It is simply the moving on and onward.

Such people, of course, have been styled spies, madmen, or at least ne'er-do-wells. All three of these distinctions have been won by the author of this book, according to the limitations or expanded imaginations of his several judges.

Sitting under the cool shelters of Chowpati on the Bombay beach, I saw the tide rolling in, and if my dejection then was not greater than that of other almost down-and-out wayfarers to be seen since on the London streets, it was in part due to a feeling that Allah does not desert those who have faith in themselves.

From the seashore I walked on, like one in a trance; my mind full of the desire to journey to Arabia. I had been ordered by my Sufi Guide to go there; and there I must go, and carry out several specific tasks in the process.

That I had almost no funds was beside the point. Allah would provide.

It was towards Crawford Bazaar that I first went, for I longed for a taste of real mangoes. They were the most innocent things of all in India. And that was a turning-point.

As I lifted a bargain basket of the luscious fruit, bought with some of my few remaining rupees in the fruit-market, I felt a soft hand on my shoulder.

'Peace upon you – fancy seeing you here!' called a voice.

Looking around, my eyes beheld a familiar face – the aide of a wealthy North Indian grandee stood before me.

The man had not changed since my days at the 'paradise of learning' at Aligarh that Sir Syed Ahmed Khan had built. Aligarh University gave that East-plus-West enlightenment that the younger generation of the Middle East was supposed to acquire in order to catch up with what is now known as the developed world.

My friend's linen cap rested just as awry as always on his well-oiled, bobbed hair. His long Mogul shirt was just as immaculately sewn with lace, and the gold buttons fastened the collar in the best accepted fashion of the Imperial Court.

2

Such was the custom of his present life; such it had been indeed, and still was – I recollected with difficulty, at my own father's court.

The aroma of his scented betel-nut wafted towards me, blotting out the days of my long stay in Europe, and recalling the years when this Prince Charming of Bhopal used to be the apple of our eyes – us, his fellow-cricketers at Aligarh.

As a courtier, he was accompanying his master on the Hajj, the pilgrimage to Holy Mecca in Arabia. The grandee had a whole pilgrim band with him. Would I join them? Would I not? Yes, I would go with them to the Cradle of Islam: and then another thought crossed my mind.

Could I, dressed as I was almost in rags, go in the entourage of a rich man, whose relatives were among the best and closest friends of my own people; of the same social circle.

And travel in third-class, (even if I could raise the money for it) whilst he occupied a first-class cabin? The snobbery of Asia is the worst under the sun: the English class-system, which people scream about, is raving Marxist proletarian-peasant anarchy in comparison.

I would think it over. For the time being, I preferred to let it lie dormant. I might be dressed as a dervish, but inwardly I was unaltered indeed from the spoilt brat I had been for years.

There were but two days to decide the question. The next afternoon I walked to the palace of a rich Indian lady – some six miles uphill from Bombay itself – to seek some inspiration on this vexed question. After all, I had an introduction to her; our families regarded one another as respectable . . .

When I arrived on the terrace of the Begum, the glamour of the afternoon garden party diminished very considerably.

She had known me when I was a rich man in Delhi society: and now, as I stepped onto her sun-bedazzled terrace, crowded with the élite of the city, there was noticeable surprise at my Indian disguise; and, no doubt, over my impoverished condition. I had, after all, been working my way here for some weeks, and work is scarce and not overpaid in India.

To be fair to her, she hardly expected to see a one-time immaculately dressed member of a diplomatic Mission step into her wondrous castle in Eastern dress – and of such a poor sort. In India they love what are considered absurd clichés today in Britain. Clothes, there, make the man!

Still, for some reason I did not think it necessary to apologise for being what I was, or for seeming to be something else. For their part, the cream of Bombay society rallied round well.

Tea was passed to me by a very delicate young Prince, who spoke with a considerable lisp. He wished to make sure I knew that he was going to England soon. He did not forget to tell me that it would be his seventeenth visit. And, of course, he always travelled first-class. I was informed, too, that he invariably stayed in Mayfair.

I met the Prince later in London, when he kindly invited me to tea in his rooms near a gasworks somewhere in the neighbourhood of Tooting. I naturally did not remind him of our former conversation on the very exclusive, rather different, terrace from which you could see miles of angry sea howling to the Malabar hills. In London, my mission complete, I was better dressed than in Bombay. He was worse accoutred, having lost all his allowance through an unwise friendship. He had not, however, been to a British public school for nothing. 'Gone up in the world?' he sneered; though not before he had prudently borrowed a sixpence for the gas meter.

There was, of course, a great lady there, an Indian lady of great age and greater proportions. Neither of these two attributes were we permitted to note. It was enough that she was an Indian Knight's wife; and, of course, we were invited to note 'how well her English pronunciation resembled that of real English women.' Whispering this, the Prince seemed almost overcome by the excitement of it all.

To my left sat someone described as a Professor, a mere youth both in age and learning, if one were to compare him with such as carried that title elsewhere in the world.

He made sure that I would never forget that he was a man of learning; so learned, indeed, that he had written a whole book. And so essential was it to benefit mankind by his scholarship that he had published it at his own expense.

The book was about the treatment of dog-bites, and in addition he was a lecturer on fine art or music, I really forget which.

But I am not wrong in recollecting that he did try, even during those short minutes when I was having my fourth cup of tea, to establish some sort of connection between the subject of his lectures and the theme of his 'well-known' book, as he put it.

He, too, was reputed to speak with a distinguished English accent; 'just like a Sahib' was the term used by the highly-impressed socialites.

I emphasise this aping of English dress and speech in an essentially Oriental gathering because it goes to show how little the deep anti-Western feeling which coexists with it has changed things. They were even thus at the height of the Gandhian 'Quit India!' Movement; and this reception was within a few miles of where the Mahatma was operating at full blast.

In the midst of this élite and glittering gathering sat I: a solitary figure in humble, very unbejewelled, Eastern dress – and with an unshaven chin.

In a country of the East, I was at least a bit of an outsider. And, affected by the society capers, my mind did not concentrate any better, and my plans for getting a ticket were no farther advanced, when I went home.

Came the day of decision. I rose from my bed still hesitant about my plans. That day, too, was the last on which I could have free lodging in the indigent travellers' rest-house.

Presently, by accident or by some providential design, I heard a great deal of shouting going on under my dormitory window. Looking out, all I could see was a medley of bazaar people, engaged in some fierce altercation. Nothing draws me like a magnet more readily than a free-for-all. Within a few minutes I had joined the throng.

An Uzbek of Central Asia, who wore long felt boots in that dreadful heat, and was undoubtedly a pilgrim on his way to Mecca, had bought a melon, and the melon was not ripe. At least, it was not as sweet as those of his Golden Samarkand; and the fruit-seller had refused to exchange it for another.

The poor Turkestani pilgrim could not make himself understood in the barbaric language of Hindustan. Not that he would have had much better luck in Urdu or Hindi: even street-hawkers in Bombay may prefer to speak what they call English rather than any Eastern tongue.

Indeed, very many Bombayites do speak only English: and there are numerous Hindus, Moslems, Parsis and Christians there who actually know almost nothing about their own religion or country. Intellectuality is what counts; being a writer or critic: and cocking a snook at traditional ideas.

How the blood tingles upon hearing your native language in far-off lands! The Uzbek, by default, was hollering in Dari-Persian at the top of his voice when I intervened. He welcomed me like a long-lost brother, suggesting that we draw our knives and show these Indians what real men were like – and much more of the same.

But I translated his complaint from Persian into Hindi, and the matter was soon adjusted; we only had to show the very points of our daggers and the crowd and the melon-man were wonderfully calmed.

Now the son of old Asia clasped me in his arms as if I were his only kin. Then he related to me the story which had hurried his steps Mecca-wards. His beloved wife had died. He could not live alone. The pain of that separation clutched him like a living vice . . . and so dearly it was that he had loved her.

The man was almost incoherent recounting the memory of his loss by the time he had finished his life-story – or, at least, the only part of his story which mattered to him.

Once his lifetime mate, friend and companion had gone, he could not live alone, he wanted to die; and what better place to reside in waiting for death than Mecca, the cradle of his faith? Thus, too, he thought to fulfil his covenant with God, by performing a pilgrimage at least once in his lifetime, as enjoined upon all the faithful.

And that, indeed, is the true spirit of the religious East; where life's bitterness arises or diminishes with one's associations. Where such associations are deeply embedded in family connections or the feeling of a husband for his wife, and *vice versa*.

In cruder form, too, you will find it in the once rife practice of *suttee*, when widows threw themselves on the burning pyre of their dead husbands.

This variety of the love of Asia still resides amongst her unsophisticated sons; amongst the ploughboys in the heart of the country born, or in the camel-train leader whose caravan winds in and out of the mighty passes of the Afghan highlands. It is one of those emotions which, like a rich stone, is best set plain. And it was in this spirit that I heard the story of the Uzbek that burnt in his heart.

That story could also combat the belief that woman in the East is a mere chattel. Actually, she is greatly respected and honoured, often infinitely more so than in Europe. What peasant youth in the West would become a hermit if he lost his spouse?

Some in the West would say, of course, that such a thing could even be considered madness.

When I rose from the Turkoman rug which my Uzbek friend had spread for me in the the rest-house, I walked towards the sea-shore, to be almost as deeply affected as I had been with the Central Asian story. It was past the time of the afternoon prayer, and the Chowpati beach was already getting crowded.

Parsi women in incredibly costly saris of wondrous hues and silken texture walked to and fro. Many sickly-looking menfolk – said to be of too-inbred stock – with pinched cheeks, wearing black velvet pillbox caps, led children behind their ladies.

A hundred or more men and women clustered around a

magician, who professed to swallow half-a-dozen razors at one gulp; the betel-nut seller smeared a lime paste on his leaves and handed them to a couple of north Indian youths.

The cool-drink seller was pouring out red and yellow and green sherbet from several bottles for those who could afford to pay a halfpenny for a glass. And, of course, there was a political lecturer with a fair number of listeners and interrupters.

Every one of the local beach trains which passed at seven-minute intervals, brought more Parsi women, more children, more cool-drink sellers. There were more betel-nut sellers, more simpering youths with motorcycles and slicked hair, their 'European' suits too tight, their smiles too loose.

Well before sundown, the whole beach seemed one seething mass of humanity and a gigantic seaside fair. I was told that it was like this on every day of the year.

This was all very well: but there was still no progress towards a ticket for the pilgrim ship. Fate had not intervened, nor shown me any direction. 'Trust in Allah,' the Prophet said, 'but tie your camel first.' Very well.

I needed somewhere to stay for the night, even if I were casting myself upon divine mercy and provision.

I made my way to a forlorn caravanserai in the less aristocratic depths of the city, where the innkeeper told me that it would cost me more than a rupee and a half to secure a night's rest. I did not wish to waste that sum, equal to a whole day's wage for a labourer, and about nine-tenths of my total worth at the time.

It would have to be the House of God. So to an adjoining mosque I betook myself. A small tin box – one of those cheap and garishly-decorated atrocities which you often see at rustic fairs – was my sole item of luggage.

However, it was late that night before the final resolution came to me regarding further travels. The previous day's meeting with the Nawab's courtier, and the story of the Uzbek, heightened my craving for Mecca. I would go, even though I did not know how.

Late though it was, and prompted by I know not what, I sallied forth to seek the residence of my Nawab friend. On no account could I ask the Prince to pay my fare: yet I had no other ideas, either.

As the proverb says: 'In movement, there is blessing'.

The palatial mansion was a tremendous hike out of the city, in a remote and expensive suburb. With that tin box perched on my turbaned head in the approved fashion of the local wayfarer, I walked a mile, two miles, four, five; and then sat down to take a rest.

The horse-carriages, the perilous-looking tramway, even the rickshaws and the cars; all were at a standstill. The city was in deep slumber as I walked through bazaar after bazaar, passed the clock-tower, the railway station, the cricket grounds. Only the occasional night patrol passed me; and yet I walked. Could I, in disguise, perhaps swell the number of the Nawab's retainers? No: I had no passport. As soon as my real name were known, I would be unmasked. Loss of face, perhaps; suspicion of criminal intent – certain . . .

The party was due to sail for Arabia precisely at 11 a.m. the following morning.

At last, in the half-light of the dawn, I saw the name-plate of the road where the Nawab's dwelling, more of a palace than a house, was situated.

At the crossroads I made a longish stop to adjust my turban, dust my shoes, pull up my socks, and to tidy myself generally before appearing even before the night watchmen of my peer. If I could not accompany him to Mecca, I could at least say prayers with him the night before he set off, and wish him Godspeed.

I moved towards the house, the unsightly tin box under my arm. That box, which I had bought in a hurry earlier in the day had, apart from its rustic floral design of lurid red and yellow, a picture of a heathen goddess with multifarious hands and feet.

This suddenly struck me as not entirely irrelevant. Fancy my possessing, flaunting, almost, that idolatrous kind of box – I, one of the Faithful, bound for the monotheistic shrine of Islam!

Thinking it over now, of course, it must have looked quite ridiculous when I stopped at the roadside at least twice, trying in the bright moonlight to rub off the figure of the pagan goddess from my Islamic luggage.

But, after all, I did have a prayer rug and a copy of the Holy Koran in it.

Now the stillness of the night was broken; the long-drawn-out chant of 'God is Greater, God is Greater' rose from the throat of the Caller, calling the faithful to the prayer of the dawn. 'Prayer is better than sleep!'

As I walked towards the minaret which marked the adjoining mosque, a small figure darted out of the darkness, pressed something into my hand, and whispered, in my own language, 'I entrust you to God', and then sped away.

Automatically I clutched the packet, which seemed like a melon-rind in paper, and put it into my tin box before hurrying into the mosque and standing in line with the Nawab's folk at prayer.

I was standing just beside His Highness in the mosque. I was expected to join his pilgrim band, of course. The

Nawab was therefore not surprised to see me, as he said when our devotions were over.

'Have you made all your arrangements?' he asked. I just smiled and thanked him for his interest. Even if it meant, as seemed likely, no pilgrimage this year, that would be better than begging from a classmate. After all, a year's work as a labourer, if I lived in mosques, might get me enough. Or two years, even. Three? Perhaps. Some people walked for longer than that to reach Mecca.

The whole entourage, naturally, had already got their tickets to the Red Sea port of Jeddah. It was of course assumed that I, too, had provided myself with one: much before that morning. After all, within a few hours all would be on board the steamer.

Then I remembered the Dari-Persian whisper, the encounter near the mosque and, yes, the melon-rind.

Wrapped in a bag which had contained a melon was a large sum in paper-money. A note said, in a Central Asian scrawl: 'Friend, brother, compatriot: go to Holy Mecca as my substitute, in accordance with Islamic custom. Pray for me there. I am too sad, not in a spiritual state of mind, to go myself. I must return to Turkestan, until my sorrow is purged. I entrust thee to Allah!'

It was signed: 'Guljanev the Uzbek, melon-eater'.

The miracle had happened.

The next two hours were among the busiest in my life. I had to get a ticket, secure a passport, buy some medicine, the regulation sheet to be worn on the pilgrimage and some articles of clothing.

The difficulty was that not only were the various offices and shops where I had to go, at very scattered points of the compass, but it was not at all probable that I would get accommodation on the ship. It was, of course, a pilgrim steamer in which they pack the travellers like pilchards in a tin. But the notice was, as people kept saying, 'absurdly short'. Nor could one get a passport by merely rushing into the Government Office. Indians themselves were known to call their country *Redtape-istan*.

It can therefore be imagined how I stumbled in my haste, running like a hunted thing. When I was so confused and jumpy that I could not tell them at the shipping company's office which class I wanted to travel, the booking clerk tapped me on the shoulder and took me aside: 'Take my tip . . .' and he stopped.

I took his tip, (which meant 'Give me a tip', of course) and a number of rupees slipped from my hand into his.

Luckily I acquired the tipping skill early on in my frantic travels around Bombay; and so I soon realised that I needed a large part of the Uzbek's donation to bribe the police and passport office, the port authorities, the health people, and so on.

As one worthy put it to me: 'In India, backsheesh is democratic: everyone, large and small, takes it.' He wasn't lying, as the Kabulis put it.

I was travelling first-class, since nothing else was left: but I soon found that the pilgrim ships' first-class was worse than even tourist-third in most liners. The pilgrim traffic was one of the most lucrative and cynical of Bombay industries.

As I emerged from the booking-office like a veritable whirlwind, a typical oily local clerk noticed my tin box.

Eyeing it, he said, in that sibilant voice that portends, well, bribery, hereabouts: 'Sahib, I note faint trace of Black Mother Goddess Kali picture painted on your case. She is the one I pray to daily in temple.'

He assumed a look of the greatest piety, his loincloth almost slipping off as he put his palms together in an attitude of the most profound prayer. I had already learnt that day that these types were the worst.

'And of course I need box just like that to remind me of her when I am not at temple. But I cannot afford one. Is that not too much sad? And also other sadness may come. For instance, I would not like it, Sahib, if it were found that your ticket had some irregularity. You wouldn't be able to catch ship, isn't it?' The prayer-rug under my arm was all I needed now; that and the Koran in its cotton bag slung over my shoulder. I pressed the box on the pious extortioner and, ignoring his heartfelt prayers that Holy Mother Kali would requite my spontaneous spiritual present, raced through an enveloping dust-cloud towards the Hajj ship.

Presently, what looked like thousands of people, a concourse of humanity, emptied itself from a train onto an adjoining jetty in front of me.

They were all making for a huge tin shed, the blazing sun of the tropics beating upon their shaven heads. All we pilgrims were to be vaccinated under that red-hot roof.

In row upon row we sat waiting for the doctor to arrive: Afghans, Persians, Javanese, Indians and Malays. There were Albanians and Yugoslavs, Chinese from Sinkiang, Chechens, Georgians, Siamese, Arabs, all staring at one another and often trying to follow languages few of us had ever heard before.

At last the vaccination was done. No sooner was the medical certificate grabbed and our fellow pilgrims free to move, than one could see some of them hurrying along a passage with the left shirt-sleeve still rolled up.

A moment later they were behind the shed, washing the scratch inflicted by the vaccinator. According to the rumour in many far-off villages of ancient Asia, the lymph used in its manufacture is considered to be 'an impurity of the cow', and such rumours in the East die hard.

At the quay lay the ship to Jeddah, and when the final word to depart was given by the medical authorities, there was a rush for the gangway.

Stalwart Pathans of the frontier, weak and ill-fed Bengalis, slant-eyed men of Bokhara, veiled women with children in their arms; all made one great rush.

They lugged their valuables along with them in sacks, crudely-made boxes, or bulging baskets insecurely tied with ropes. The sacks, however, were in predominance; labelled as items of 'Portable Luggage', always 'Wanted on Voyage'.

We, the faithful, were excited, more truly excited than children before a party, for an emotional veil hung over the whole scene. We were bound for a city the thought of which had been with us since childhood; a city of holy dreams and devout yearning; almost in the blood of every Moslem – a part of a tradition thirteen centuries old.

And the noise and bustle blended with the sanctified air of the pilgrim ship. We rushed the gangway, people colliding with sacks; bundles and baskets pushing into people; a clay water-jar now peeping out of a sack, now pushed up by the jostling crowd, and then slipping out of the hands of its owner into the sea.

Thus the narrow pathway of the gangplank led the faithful to the deck and away down into the ship's enormous, cavernous depths.

Three shrill blasts, the thud of the engines, and slowly we moved away from the shore amid cries of 'God is Greater, God is Greater'.

Existence on the pilgrim ship, to one used to the ordinary comforts of life, was, to say the least, harassing. Although much had recently been done by the Saudi

Government to provide better conditions, the devotees were appallingly jampacked, crowded together.

The worst phase of the voyage began on the third day, for practically every pilgrim was now in the throes of *mal-de-mer*. One of them: a cleric who only the day before had told me that he could never be seasick (due to his great piety), was in the very worst straits. Totally prostrated, he prayed loudly, earnestly and incessantly for God to send death to release him.

Then the shouting and the harrowing scenes came to a standstill, but morale was low. The sky was now grey, the wind swept the vessel, and the waves beat on the sides with more than ordinary force. The pilgrims, though more accustomed to the motion, still hated the sight of the waves.

Corpse-like figures lay on the deck, on their sacks of cooking-charcoal, on coiled ropes, everywhere, uttering not a word, hardly interested in existence and avoiding any food or drink. Many thought an evil spirit had come upon the boat.

But it takes more than a rough sea to suspend life altogether, for as soon as the waves subsided the corpse-like ones rolled up their bedding, sat up and cooked their food. The Persians made tea, the Bengalis skinned fish, the Pathans were busy with their pilau rice of excellent flavour.

During the spell of seasickness, the pilgrims had lost all clear idea of their purpose; but on recovering they soon remembered the solemn idea that induced them to journey to the city of their childhood and lifelong prayers.

The atmosphere on the boat was suddenly thick with religion; prayer rugs and mats were spread, recitations of the Koran were chanted, doctors of theology were busy reading to the devotees those chapters of the Moslem Holy

Book which related to that part of the journey of the pilgrimage.

In the afternoon, religious discussions took place, and even political ones: though both would usually end where they began. Thus the life of the pious on a pilgrim ship was spent, until one day, soon after dawn, the captain appeared on the deck and pointed out to us in the distance a dark blue line – the Holy Land of Islam! The Arabian coast! The port of Jeddah!

I could hardly speak for excitement, for was I not going to see that great unknown towards which I had stretched out my hands all my life?

Little by little it became clearer, as we stood watching it in our regulation pilgrim costume, until the white city of minarets and domes – Jeddah – lay as if cut in marble, when the boat dropped anchor some two miles from the shore.

From that point no ship could go nearer, as the reefs are very treacherous, and we crossed to the jetty in tiny sailing-boats, tossing like cockle-shells on the crest of the waves.

The first sight of Jeddah gripped me with a strange feeling of an end and a beginning. I gazed at it as a Moslem, with pleasure mingled with awe and reverence. Beyond that city, fifty miles or so away, lay Mecca, the goal of my hopes – the Holy of Holies of every Moslem.

Life's dream, I thought, had at last been realised. The tautness of the muscles of my face and those tears which dimmed my eyes were indications of my emotions.

The scene was strangely familiar, for had I not faced the Holy City, seeing it in my mind's eye five times every day in prayer? Absorbed in these thoughts, I remained in Jeddah for the night, and next day started towards Mecca.

Those of us who had more money than sense were

bundled into a large motor-car, and were told that by this means we could best travel the fifty miles inland. We had not gone far when a halt was called at the reputed tomb of Eve. Curious as to the grave of my great ancestress, I alighted to examine it.

She must have been a lady of formidable proportions, for the original grave, I was told, was some eight feet long. But the plot had, by the time I arrived, mysteriously extended itself to altogether gigantic dimensions.

On payment of a fee, I learned that, during the old days, one could receive an oracular message from the buried progenitress of suffering humanity. This was, of course, supplied by a confederate of the tomb-keeper in an underground crypt, who, for a silver thaler or two, droned out a 'prophecy'. Fortunately, this evil practice was stopped by the advent of the Saudis, whose puritan Wahabi sect had swept down from Nejd in the north, onto this, the Hejaz region, when they conquered the peninsula.

As we trundled over the sandy tracts, we felt the grilling heat of the desert overpoweringly. I was dressed in the traditional 'sheet' which actually consists of two sheets, one for the upper part of the body, the other for the lower; knotted together as pins or sewing are frowned on for pilgrim garb by Moslem law. In accordance with immemorial custom, too, my head was shaved and unprotected from the merciless sun.

At last, after twenty-five miles of the hottest journey that I have ever known, we halted at the half-way house of Bahra, where we were told there was a well. Thanks to the Wahabi King Abdul-Aziz, we found not only water, but even cool drinks – heaven-sent in the scorching heat of the desert.

Hardly had we journeyed three miles beyond the well when the rear wheels of our car sank deep in a sand-dune.

We alighted and strove to move the venerable and
ancient vehicle, but to no purpose, and much to the
contemptuous amusement of a passing Bedouin, who
from the back of his swift-trotting camel jeered at us
unmercifully.

'It serves you right for bringing that creation of Satan
into the sacred land,' he yelled. 'Why can't you travel on
camel-back, like other folk? See, I can make my camel
stop when I want and go when I wish him to. Take that
iron contraption back to the devil who made it.' He hauled
us out, entirely by camel-power, now roaring with laughter at our red faces.

From the moment the pilgrim enters Mecca to the time
of his departure, he is kept in a fever of excitement and
pious frenzy. Ceremony after ceremony claims his constant and unfaltering attention. For hours, he is wedged in
by swaying and seething crowds.

One of the rites is to pass seven times between the places
called Safa and Marwa, the alleged tombs of Hagar and
Ishmael, a distance of perhaps three hundred yards, which
is known as the Sai ceremony, and from which one may
acquire much merit. The road is not narrow, but is constantly crowded with pilgrims. Add to this, prayers five
times a day, and there is not much time to see the sights of
Mecca. Not that there is really much to see in the non-
religious sense of the term; the atmosphere of the town is
austere – and so, indeed it should be. The Saudi Wahabis,
the guardians of the Holy Shrines, had banned any action
or even display which conflicted with the austerity of
Islam.

Before the actual day of the pilgrimage and before
attending the assembly of the Grand Moslem Conference,
I had time to make occasional excursions in and around
the city of Mecca. Walking right through it, the actual

town cannot be more than two and a half miles long; beyond Babal Umra there are quite delightful houses of modern construction and with an adequate water supply. But the heart of Mecca is the Great Mosque, the Harem Sharif, in the centre of which stands the stone structure known as the Kaaba, The Cube. The Black Stone, which every pilgrim kisses, is built into one of its walls.

During my 40,000 miles or more of travelling by land and sea, both in the East and the West, I had not so far come upon a building with which I could compare the Great Mosque in Mecca. In design and style the structure has no parallel. Essentially, it is a great rectangular court-yard, about 250 yards long and a little less than this in width. Nineteen gateways give access to its interior; entering it a remarkable spectacle strikes upon the eyes. All around are colonnades crowned with rather low arch-shaped domes. Several minarets rise from the walls.

From various points along the outer colonnades, narrow pathways lead to the centre of the space where stands the Kaaba entirely draped in a thick black tapestry with gold-embroidered extracts from the Koran running in a band towards the top.

Nearby is the well of Zam Zam, reputed to have yielded water to Hagar. Then there are pulpits from which prayers are conducted, because pilgrims in prayer while actually inside the Great Mosque surround the stone structure of the Kaaba; and a great congregation of the Islamic world meets there five times a day.

The prayers take place at dawn, midday, afternoon, sunset and at night. All Moslems face towards Mecca in their devotions. When actually in Mecca, they face towards the Great Mosque. When in the Mosque, they surround the Kaaba, facing any one of its four walls.

And now as to the spirit which grips one in Mecca.

When I was on this journey, I had already lived in or had contact with the dazzling civilisation of the West for about ten years. I loved comfort. While I could rough it on a journey, as most Orientals can, yet the lack of physical well-being in this city distressed me at first; that is, the veneer of Europe lay thick on me. I was not the most devout of Moslems, nor indeed was I over-conscious of the power of religion. There was a good deal of 'alloy in my heart', as the Sufis put it.

With this mental attitude I entered Mecca, expecting iced water, electric fans, sumptuously decorated apartments, good motor-cars and more.

Instead I found a temperature of over 133 degrees in the shade, no mechanical means of locomotion, strange food, very little ice, and apartments but poorly furnished. In fact, I met with every discomfort which one could fairly easily remedy outside Mecca.

But now a strange feeling came upon me. I found myself suddenly dropping into a sort of mental vacuum. Discomforts did not feel such. And if I did not pray, and pray in the grilling heat of the Great Mosque, I felt most wretched.

Everything else beyond Mecca, outside that quadrangle with its Kaaba, was lost to me – I literally forgot everything outside. All day long, all night too, I did nothing, cared to do nothing else but pray, bending and kneeling towards that mysterious and august stone building, standing as it did, draped in black. I slept on the stone floor of the Mosque, and used to get up and bathe for prayer at all sorts of odd hours of the night.

Nor was I alone in this practice; for every minute of the day and night people were reading the Koran, or bending low in prayer, or going around and around the Kaaba building, dazed as if by some indefinable influence.

But it is to be noted regretfully that the atmosphere changed when one went a little further away from the Great Mosque. One incident stands out clearly in my mind.

The Maulvi Mohamed Ali and his brother, Maulvi Shaukat Ali – at the time giants of Indian politics – were staying in Mecca, awaiting the opening of the World Moslem Conference which the Wahabi King had convened. They were delegates and I was an observer.

My visit to their lodgings to inquire after the health of the Mohamed Ali – who had been ill – and my reception there may prove how true is the saying that even in Mecca people may behave in an unholy manner. It is widely believed, incidentally, that the influence of the Holy City corresponds to the reverence in which one truly holds it.

When I arrived at the apartment of the Maulvis, I found them lolling about on cushions, and engaged in a fierce argument with the Palestinian delegates about the alleged atrocities of the Wahabi King.

That they were the guests of that King in Mecca may not be beside the point. Upon my taking my seat at the end of the room, a silence fell upon the company. A silence which menaced: for I knew that these Mullahs had never favoured my line of policy. In spite of my youth, they were well aware of it, and spared no opportunity to denounce me. It should be observed that they spared nobody whose opinion differed from theirs in the least degree. They looked upon each other as venerable authorities and sat brooding over vanished glories, when an insignificant man like me dared to challenge their opinion. At last, grimacing like an ogre, the younger brother spoke – to the Grand Mufti of Jerusalem:

'This man,' he said, pointing to me, 'this youth, is one of our most brilliant men of Islam, but he likes the British and,' he sneered, 'whether he loves Islam or the British more, I do not know.'

I could not control my temper, and in a spirited reply reminded him that he had misunderstood me all along, and that he was a little too concerned about losing his self-fashioned crown at the hands of younger people, whilst at no time would I sell myself for anybody's friendship.

The other brother took the words out of the mouth of one, Sulaiman Nadir, and taunted me for taking a wife from a different clan than my own, as if that were a matter of Islamic importance.

It is strange, though, how both taunts came home to roost. The younger Maulvi, in public and before witnesses, in London and in tears, begged the British during the Indian Round Table Conference, to bury him in their own country – in the land for the lifeblood of whose people he had thirsted until only a year or two before.

His brother was later married to a young and virtuous English girl; hardly a member of his clan.

I did not mention, did I, that when I returned to my accustomed place on the floor of the Grand Mosque, I recounted what had passed to two Sufi sages, who sat by the Bab Ibrahim?

One said: 'As they regard it a sin to be friends with the British, and appear to hate them: it may well be that at least one of them may one day be compelled to seek British mercy.'

The other Sufi then said: 'It could well happen that an Indian Moslem might abhor the mixing of blood, infected as he is with the accursed racial superiority feelings of that country. And so it may come to pass that an Indian might even marry an English lady, after once thinking that such an act would demean him.'

2

Mecca and Beyond

Avoiding any further contact with the political atmosphere around the Great Mosque, I prepared for the World Moslem Conference, which I had been instructed to attend, should I succeed in reaching Mecca in time for it.

The date of the inauguration was altered no fewer than three times, and it was a great relief when at last we were informed that the Islamic Conference, would begin on Sunday, June 6th, at two o'clock. It was to be held in the old Turkish artillery fortification, on the top of a rocky eminence outside the western gate of the city.

As we approached it, I noticed the green Wahabi flag flying from the tower, with the inscription in Arabic in white: 'There is no god but God, and Mohamed is his Prophet'.

Standing alone on grey rocks, the white fort presented a beguiling picture, reminding one of an Arabian knight's castle from the Middle Ages. All around the building, on the rocky ground, earth had been spread and sown with barley and other cereals to produce a green effect like a lawn, and a dozen or so men were spraying water on the young shoots.

At the entrance, white-robed officials wearing white turbans received us and examined our credentials. Then we passed up the wide staircase to the hall upstairs where the Congress was to deliberate – a spacious oblong apartment some ninety feet in length. There were latticed wooden shutters to the window openings painted green, this also being the colour of the curtains and the covers on the tables. The latter were arranged in the form of two giant horseshoes with a fair space between them.

Most of the leading Moslem countries were represented though the Turkish delegates failed to make an appearance until later: for Turkey had only recently become a secular State. The USSR had seven delegates; the Hejaz twelve; Java five; India twelve; Nejd five; Asir three; Palestine three, and Syria three. In addition to these, the Wahabi King had arranged for two doctors of theology to appear for the Sudan and three to represent Egypt. In addition to Turkey, neither Iraq nor the Yemen was represented at the Conference until later. The Persians, whose country was one of the very few Islamic ones which was fully independent, never came at all.

Precisely at two o'clock, when all had taken their seats, a muffled explosion shook the building. It was the firing of the salute from the fort announcing that the King was on his way to open the Congress.

'The Sultan! The Sultan!' shouted the usher.

We rose to our feet and saw about a dozen black guards wearing red tunics, white breeches and black knee boots, with the customary drawn swords, ascend the steps, followed by King Abdul-Aziz Ibn al Saud himself, accompanied by his son the Emir Faisal. Behind them were his ministers, military officials and another bodyguard.

The King went first to the antechamber just behind the President's chair and then took his seat in the middle of the hall at the President's desk. His Chief Secretary,

Sheikh Hafiz Wahaba, later Saudi Ambassador in London, stood on his right and read the King's Speech:

'I welcome you, my fellow-brothers of Islam and I am thankful that you have accepted my invitation to join this Congress, the first of its kind in Islamic history. I hope and pray to Almighty God that year by year we shall assemble to discuss our various problems. In the past there has been no such thing as Islamic public opinion. Islam has lacked the spirit of reformation and uplift. The government of the Hejaz has been administered by Caliphs or Sultans, who paid little attention to the question of the betterment of this country. There were other Islamic rulers with good intentions who, on account of their illiteracy and lack of knowledge, showed their incapacity to do good to Arabia. Wealthy men, who cared nothing for the future of this country, gave licence and liberty to the people here to such an extent that in this holy and sacred city un-Islamic practices became rife and disturbances began all over the country. Some of the governors of this country have been severe both to the pilgrims and to the inhabitants of this city.

'After the decline of Turkish rule in Arabia, when the government fell into the hands of Sherif Husein and his son Ali, the whole Islamic world became uneasy on account of their inability to govern this sacred land, and every Moslem became anxious concerning the future peace and prosperity of the country. Official papers which have fallen into our hands justify our statement that its late rulers had handed over the independence of the country to foreigners and that they were in their pay. We, the people of Nejd, being the neighbours of the Hejaz, were particularly affected by the cruelties of Husein. He regarded us as infidels and prohibited us from performing our religious pilgrimage to Mecca. Not only did he do this, but he was instrumental in fanning discontent among my subjects of Nejd. When the limit to these cruelties and depredations had been reached and my Ministers and compatriots satisfied me that it was my religious duty to protect Islam from such evils, then, relying upon God and God's support alone, I did not spare my life and property and money to achieve that end. God gave us victory and helped us to purge the sacred land of its oppressors and enabled us, the people of Nejd, to fulfil our promise towards the people of Islam.

'I further fulfilled that promise by inaugurating this International Moslem Congress, and in my invitation to you I spoke of my personal views regarding the future government of the Hejaz. My first invitation received no response, except from our brothers in India. Though disappointed I issued a second which I am glad to see has borne fruit. You can see with your own eyes that not only are the various sacred places and shrines in the Hejaz safe, but their sanctity is being preserved and these dearly-beloved places are being duly protected. For the first time for many generations there is peace in the land and perfect security to the pilgrim. This state of peace and tranquillity I mean to maintain according to the strict injunctions of Islam. I invited you to this assembly to discuss and explore avenues for the moral and religious betterment of the Hejaz which may be satisfactory to God and man alike. This Government is being run on the lines of the Koran and is free from the vices which had crept into the general practices of the people. I request you to discuss these points. I desire you to make up the deficiency in the morals of the people and to make this sacred land the real fount and cradle of goodness and civilisation, of health and goodwill. Almost everything in this country requires some betterment, and in the betterment of the people of the

Hejaz every Moslem must help. My brothers, you are a free people gathered together in this assembly to give free expressions of your views. Islam's weakness today is the wrangling between various sects, which is contrary to the dictates of the Holy Book. And I beg of you to discover means of obtaining a cohesion of ideas and the lowering of those barriers that keep heart from heart. I pray God that He may guide you and me to a serious solution of these difficult problems. May peace be with you.'

The speech was heard in silence. The King rose, bowed to right and left, gave his greetings, went to his antechamber and returned to his palace, with his guards following him, while all stood.

We were left in a dilemma as to the mode of procedure. As the King had said, we had never had an international Islamic conference before.

Hafiz Wahaba proposed that, for the time being, the oldest delegate should occupy the presidential chair and conduct the business till a permanent president should be elected and this honour fell to Maulvi Abdul Wahid.

He read a long passage from the Koran after which Mohamed Ali, the delegate of the Caliphate Committee from India,(the man who had shortly before attacked me for such crimes as my marriage and being a British spy and stooge) rose and said it was very regrettable that brothers in Islam – namely the Turks and the Arabs – had been set against one another in that holy city as a result of the revolt of the Arabs against the Turks during the War, largely engineered by the mischievous activities of Husein and his followers.

Now that the reconstruction of Islamic interests was being effected through the agency of that assembly he thought it only right and fitting that the head of the

Turkish delegation should be made president, in order to cement the *rapprochement* between the peoples of the Islamic world.

Evidently our temporary president, Maulvi Abdul Wahid, could not tolerate this, the more so as no Turkish delegate was present. Jumping to his feet and shaking with old age and emotion, he declared that the suggestion of Mohamed Ali was calculated to widen the fissure and break up the friendly attitude of Moslem peoples. And when he went on to hint that Mohamed Ali was actuated by personal desires, Ali's elder brother as well as other Indian delegates, jumped up and protested vehemently against the charge. There was general consternation and an interchange of uncomplimentary remarks.

Had not someone judiciously hinted that this was a serious gathering of responsible men assembled to solve certain vexed problems and not a vegetable market, matters might have descended to abuse and blows.

The election of President resulted in the victory of Sherif Adnana who secured forty-four votes. Hafiz got one vote and the head of the non-existent Turkish delegation nine. There were some blanks.

Generally speaking, many people were glad to welcome Sherif Adnana because he was a man of sober ideas. He had been an exile for some years and had only recently returned to his home, and he was liked by everybody.

Then came the election of two vice-presidents, wherein the Seyyid Suleiman Nadvi secured thirty-two votes and Raz-ed-Din thirty. The former was the chairman of the Caliphate Committee in India and the latter, leader of the delegates from the USSR.

When it was announced that the election of a secretary-general would take place, Mohamed Ali rose on a point of order. Hitherto the Congress had been conducted in

Arabic, and to the surprise of everyone Mohamed Ali spoke in English.

This was strange, for the Ali brothers had declared time and again in India that, as well as the British Government, the English language was to be boycotted.

Amid some confusion, it was discovered that the great leader of the tens of millions of Indian Moslems could not express himself in the Holy Tongue of Arabic: and there was some curiosity as to exactly what a 'point of order' was. And whether such a point was an Islamic, or a British, invention.

The sudden introduction, at such a gathering and in such a place, of the tongue of what the Indians were continuously telling the Arabs was an 'infidel' race – in the mouth of a devout and prayerful Moslem divine, one who was an avowed enemy of the British: it was, to say the least, extraordinary in the eyes of those present.

One of the Arab delegates quickly interrupted the rather excited Maulvi, declaring that if he could not speak in Arabic, the real language of Islam, he had better express himself in Hindustani or whatever language he knew which was not that of his enemies, and an interpreter would be found.

But Mohamed Ali continued in English, after claiming that he spoke English because it was the language of a 'People of the Book', the English Christians, even though they were his enemies. He refused to speak Urdu, his native tongue, because, he said, it was known by millions of 'unclean Hindus, idol-worshippers . . .'

Having been given permission to continue in the Book People's language, the Maulvi wanted to know on what basis the delegates had been elected. Indian representatives, he declared, should be entitled to more votes than those of Nejd or Asir, because they represented an infinitely larger body of Moslems. When his remarks were translated, there was much talk and whispering among those on the President's right where sat the representatives of Nejd, Asir, the Hejaz and Syria. They did not wish to accept that there was anything in Mohamed Ali's contention. They failed to understand how he dared to make such a proposal, breaching etiquette to such a disastrous degree, in such an assembly.

He wanted, they said, to differentiate between Moslem and Moslem. He was seeking self-advertisement and self-aggrandisement, which the restive independence and individualism of the Arab cannot brook.

Voting papers were then handed round, but once more Mohamed Ali rose and inquired of the President what had become of his proposal. There was no reply, and when he realised he was being ignored he made another suggestion turning the tables completely.

'We in India,' he said, 'are slaves; we are not independent, our necks are bleeding under the hobnails of the English. We cannot justifiably claim to have equal status with the free people of Nejd or the Hejaz. I propose, therefore, that if we Moslems in India have one vote, then the people of independent countries should have four.'

Perhaps he thought this would please the Arabs. But, like the preceding proposal, nobody made any comment. Taufiq Sherif was elected secretary-general by an overwhelming majority.

Next day the real work began. The first item was that the assembly be called the 'All-World Moslem Congress'; that it be held yearly in Mecca during the time of the pilgrimage. Here Mohamed Ali rose to propose an amendment.

'Supposing there is war in Arabia,' he said, 'and the

31

delegates could not get to Mecca; where is the assembly to sit?'

After some discussion, it was decided that if there were war or disturbances in Mecca then the Congress would meet in some independent Islamic country where Islamic law was practised; failing such a country, then in the best possible Islamic province.

Another proposal was to purchase the buildings surrounding the Great Mosque, knock them down, and make a wide avenue right around the Holy Place. This led to very heated discussion. The majority of the delegates favoured it; but apparently not a few had vested interests in the properties concerned.

However, it was referred to a committee with instructions that it should go thoroughly into the question, draw up plans, and advise the Government of the Hejaz on the subject.

One of the most far-reaching schemes, which was duly carried after three days' discussion, was the proposal to build a railway line between Jeddah and Mecca and link it with the Hejaz Railway at Medina, and also to construct a branch line to Yanbu, the port of Medina. It was also agreed to carry out certain essential improvements at the port of Rabegh, on the Red Sea, south of Yanbu. A harbour was to be built and docking accommodation provided.

An interesting feature of the railway proposal was that the money for the construction of the line was to be provided by general subscription throughout the various Islamic countries and when the undertaking was completed and running, half of the revenue was to go to the Hejaz Government and the other half to the upkeep of the line.

'Why half the proceeds should go to the Government,

when the Arabs were not prepared to spend a penny on it can best be answered by the Wahabi King himself,' added Mohamed Ali.

There was an outcry at this further infraction of good behaviour; but the Arabs have a great sense of humour. A sheikh from Medina restored everyone's good temper, in a doubtless unconscious imitation of the true parliamentary manner, by suggesting that the Indian be forgiven, 'since he was clearly suffering from the unfortunate effects of what he had earlier described as the condition in his country: British hobnails on his neck!'

Other resolutions passed included the decision to establish hospitals and base camps where pilgrims making the Haj could obtain medical attention and comforts; and finally it was agreed that from next year, every delegate must contribute towards the running expenses of the Congress.

The spirit of good fellowship which existed at the Conference was, however, marred in its later phase when the Ali brothers sharply questioned Wahabi practices.

Many of the customs which were resorted to by the ignorant pilgrims, especially Indians, run contrary to the true spirit of Islam; and these the Wahabis rightly prohibited, thus giving an opportunity to the Ali brothers to raise a storm on that score. Not only did they want to have the repair and guardianship of the shrines in the hands of a body of which they would be a part: they also urged that all fees collected from the pilgrims should be disbursed by the nominees of the Conference; which was clearly transgressing the laws of hospitality and an interference in the sovereignty of the Wahabi Kingdom – which even a far lesser man than the redoubtable Abdul-Aziz Ibn Saud would never have tolerated.

Throughout, there was an extraordinary demonstration

of cultural differences, when the continuous interruptions and adversarial habits of the people of the Indian sub-continent – which they found perfectly normal at home – were met with a wall of silent disapproval from grave-faced Arabs, who had seldom experienced anything like it. It was indeed a striking lesson in culture-clash.

The Conference broke up after a stormy session, for the performance of the actual pilgrimage. The full pilgrimage does not consist only of visiting Mecca; close to the Holy City at Arafat many religious ceremonies have to be performed.

On the 8th of Zilhij the pilgrims, wearing only the usual regulation costume of one white sheet, leave Mecca. Taking the Taif road, everyone journeys to the plains of Arafat; and usually a halt is called at the village of Mina after about three hours' journey from Mecca; but many continue straight on to Arafat. Crossing the landmark of Muzdalifa and the narrow rocky defiles, one comes to the Hill of Mercy, at which sacrifices are offered to complete the Haj ceremony.

Smitten with the heat and in the grip of a high fever, I left the Cradle of Islam, after completing my various duties.

Dawn was breaking; its grandeur grew lovelier and more definite as one streak of light blended with another on the ridges far away; and the two-seater car kindly supplied by the King sped on to the shores of the Red Sea.

The moving sand was like the marching of men; and, though ill in body – for I had contracted enteric fever – I had an inner feeling of exhilaration at having performed a visit to a place the like of which exists nowhere else in the world – the cynosure of Islam, the grail of every Moslem's heart.

I was advised to get out of the heat as quickly as I could; and at Jeddah, fortunately, a small craft was setting her sails. With little difficulty I got standing-room on it. The captain of the boat, though not knowing me, was willing to take a chance with a passenger in his lugger-boat as far as Port Sudan, just across the Red Sea.

The Sudanese crew looked at me almost with reverence as I stood bargaining to be taken across to their country. Though they visited Jeddah regularly, they were not able to afford the journey to Holy Mecca themselves.

Every pilgrim back from the land of the Hejaz is an object of respect and envy to these simple and lovable people of the Sudan. But I was too dazed with fever to take any notice of their congratulations on having been to the Cradle of Islam. Jumping into their somewhat unsteady rowing-boat, I bade them hasten. As to what coin I gave them for hire I do not remember; for me it was enough that I was getting to some place where I could find a bed to lie on.

There was only one hotel in Port Sudan, just facing the quay, and it was modern. They wanted to charge me a gold pound a day, and wanted it in advance. I told them I had three sovereigns in my possession. I had little hope of reaching Jerusalem, my ultimate destination, with only three coins and the enteric fever still in the marrow of my bones, the management thought. But I felt rich enough: and I was in a daze. I reeled to a room and, switching on the electric fan, I flung myself on to the bed. I knew no more till fully twenty-four hours later, and whether it was sleep or if I was comatose, I never cared to ascertain.

It was on the third day, when the management found that I could not pay in advance because I wished to retain that last coin, that I had to leave the hotel. There was not much to pack – only a prayer mat and a copy of the Koran. I possessed nothing more.

I had a belt with a large brass buckle on it, given to me by my Sufi teacher, who had drawn my attention to the symbol inscribed on it. I had half understood that this device might be recognised by others on the same spiritual path: who might help, but only when one was at the end of one's tether.

Thus it was that, overcome by heat and dehydration, I sat down in the impoverished souk of Port Sudan like any other of the many exhausted wayfarers who dotted its streets. I found under my hand a small piece of charcoal. Behind me was a whitewashed wall. On the wall I carefully drew the symbol; a sort of double-square. Then I fell asleep, or unconscious . . .

I woke with a start, to find water being splashed on my face, and a man speaking to me in Hindustani.

In conversation, I discovered that my young friend was a Borah, originally from Bombay, who traded in betelnuts, wrist watches, cloth – in fact, anything and everything which he could import from India in a small way. He thought I looked forlorn, he said, and guessed that I must be needing help. He carefully wiped the symbol of the Sufis from the wall with a clean towel, and took me to his home, where I was given food and rest for some days.

Then he took me to his warehouse. It was a barn of a place divided into two sections, an office and a store. The building was open at the back like a caravanserai. The office had no files, no pen or ink, no ledgers. All business was done by word of mouth. He did not believe in wasting his time dusting the office, because 'as soon as you dust, another sandstorm would soon make it dusty again'.

For day after day, I sat under the thatched roof in his warehouse, drinking soda-water which was quickly made by throwing handfuls of something into an earthen pot of water beside me.

Our dinner consisted of dried dates, rice and smoked and dried meat soaked in camel's fat. I helped myself liberally and liked it, chiefly because I had been living on rather short, if not non-existent, rations. The pound-a-day at the hotel did not include any food.

A few days later, a score or more Indians and others of the non-Arab population, who were either employed or were trading at Port Sudan, were invited to meet me. Dried dates and curd were served, and even the notionally vegetarian Hindu merchants were eating camel with the rest.

It was astonishing to me to hear how well these crowds of Indian Hindu shopkeepers spoke Arabic. Of course, they pronounced the words with their own Hindustani accent. They were not going to give up all their national characteristics, they said, when I enquired about intonation. Far into the night we sat, talking and gossiping about many lands and many trades. Occasionally our host had to chase a jackal away from under the floor of the huts, which were built on raised and propped-up wooden platforms.

Perhaps it was that the period of my fever was over; or it was the change in the air from Arabia to Africa; or only that Fate had ordained that I should continue to live. Anyway, I was soon better – so much better indeed, that I actually walked to the quay to see whether there was any prospect of sailing to the Near East. And there was one ship there. They were loading peanuts onto it.

For a consideration, I proposed to the man on watch that his captain might take me to a European port. I was taken before the captain.

'What do you want?' he growled at me. I explained.

'I can't,' he said, 'and I would not! Quite a lot of

scoundrels want to escape. I am not of those who will give them a lift and get into trouble for it.'

He blew hard his strawberry nose and gulped another dose of a beverage denied to me as a Moslem. I descended the gangway, very much down from my pedestal.

'Besides,' he yelled after me, 'you can speak English. Why do you not buy and sell like those blighters who are fore and aft of you?'

Buy and sell! The thought leaped into my mind.

Sheikh Umru, the local bead- and curio-merchant, had many men working for him. Why should I not sell his wares at the dockside? The Sheikh agreed, and soon provided me with beads and amulets of glass, trinkets of sorts reputedly hand-cut by the best Sudanese workmen; but in fact imported from Birmingham. Lion claws, hair from the mane of the king of the animals, made into brooches and so on in the workshop of the Sheikh, were sold to the European curio-hunters who frequently passed on British ships through Port Sudan.

When the next steamer arrived, I was all ready with dangling strings of beads, rosaries of the Holy Witch, and the claw that warded off evil.

Old and young, mostly women, crowded the rails and yelled at me to come up. My rival tradesmen were more fleet-footed than I; they had experience dating back to when they had been urchins. But the British soon found that I could make myself better understood. They clamoured to examine the wares of the native who spoke English so well.

Thus I made a good harvest. I was bringing psychology into trade. I saw a young courting couple mooning like two half-wits as they bent over the ship's railing, giggling over nothing. Approaching them, I proffered the young lady a ring of elephant hair and dilated upon its wonder-working qualities bringing good luck to the newly-wed. Only a few of that kind of ring were made by a Sudanese witch every year. That was the local belief, anyway. Its price was more than one of equal weight in gold. In fact, I could have said more in its praises, according to the Sheikh's advice but a little was sufficient and the magic ring was promptly bought.

The next customer was a missionary lady from South India. She knew the price of the junk which I carried, for it was her thirty-first voyage back to the East. But one thing she did not know – psychology. The beads she did not want; for the other bric-a-brac also she had no use; but had I a cure for baldness? I did; and the solution was none other than common salt and ammonia, slightly coloured with madder. The people of the Red Sea coast swore by it ...

A sergeant's wife, with what seemed like about nine infants hanging round her, hailed me next but seeing her encumbrances I did not break my neck to serve her; instead, I edged round to a prosperous-looking middle-aged man.

He was too wise to patronise me, and remarked to his fellow in the next deck-chair that in Dundee they could buy my entire assortment for ninepence. 'So you can! But have you seen this stamp which I have? A real Arab stamp, amazingly old?' He had not, and he bought it at a good price for his album, which had incidentally fallen from his lap as I approached him, a fact of which I had made a mental note. By the time I had finished I counted fully nine gold pounds profit on my sales – not bad for an afternoon's business. For the first time I realised the meaning of studying one's market.

It was a great evening in the annals of the Sheikh's trading days when he counted the proceeds of my afternoon's sales. We went fifty-fifty. A month of such brisk trading and I should have enough to pay for my fare to Europe on a cargo ship; so I tarried at Port Sudan, making ready for the arrival of the next steamer.

After a week's weary waiting, the next boat did arrive but there was a yellow flag floating from its mast-head. They had smallpox on board. For the next three weeks no further ship came into Port Sudan, and my Sheikhly employer found my keep rather expensive.

Then there was another intervention in my life. One dark night as I was sitting somewhat morosely in the dimly-lit shop, an employee of a shipping agency where I had enquired for a passage came to see me. He gave me enough in Egyptian money to buy a ticket to Port Said and a little over; but on one condition did he offer it.

'I am a follower of the Sufi path, a dervish,' he said, 'and not a rich man. I want to see that no deserving person is stranded and will help everyone I can: provided you will not mention my name to anybody, and do not return the sum to me, but rather make a chain of this good action. Help someone else in the manner that I have helped you.'

I was so moved with this true spirit of charity that I very nearly wept. Slipping the money into my hand he was gone, perhaps never to meet me again.

The very next day I took passage on a freighter. The sum at my disposal could not buy me anything better than deck accommodation. When I had paid even for that cheapest of all rates I had just two gold pieces left. These I tied in the corner of my handkerchief and wore it under my shirt, next to my skin.

The ship had hardly left the shore when the thought of food on the voyage distressed me. The purser could not allow any rations to be given to me for less than eight pounds; so, being at my wit's end, I had either to cook my own food with the Lascars and buy flour and butter and other items, which would cost at least three pounds up to Port Said; or fall upon the mercy of the unhelpful-looking Goanese head-waiter on the boat. I chose the latter course. He agreed to give me the left-overs from the table for a pound. The other pound I tied even more securely around my neck, for I wanted to travel beyond the Egyptian coast. Three meals I was given by the waiter.

True to the bargain, they were scraps from the table, half-pats of butter, a nibbled piece of toast, a discoloured over-sugared and discarded cold cup of tea. These delicacies were placed before me in the scullery of the dining-saloon, and them I ate voraciously, thanking God fervently for His small mercies.

In between the meals, I used to mix with my fellow-passengers on the deck.

There were eight Hindus, all bound for South America to ply some small pedlar's trade.

There was a young Indian Moslem from Kenya with his tiny son, whom he was taking to school in England. Once a rising light at Cambridge University, this young man had incurred the wrath of his conservative Indian father by marrying an English woman.

When the old gentleman cut him off with a shilling, he gallantly went as a trader to Kenya and was doing fairly well.

Then there was another rather sober-looking young Punjabi. A former Sikh, he was now an enthusiastic convert to the Christian Scientists, and was on his way to its centre in Boston.

A long and narrow passage ran along the hold in the ship, and it was there that we 'lived' during the night. All along the length of the space, iron bunks were fixed to the side of the ship. There were no port-holes, no means of breathing fresh air. You could hardly breathe at all, unless you opened the iron doors and flooded the interior with foetid air. Everybody did his cooking there, the Hindus took their baths in the place, they spread their washing there to dry, and then we all slept there.

If the Black Hole of Calcutta or a prison cell is worse than the accommodation which I am describing, then all I can say is that you should thank your stars that you have not the experience of that place which I had.

And then the greatest of all tragedies occurred.

One bright morning, while I was admiring the scenery of the coastline, the ship lurched a little; a spray of water rose high and, dashing itself against our lower deck, completely soaked us. It was easy to dry myself merely by donning the pilgrim sheet. During this operation of changing however, I must somehow have loosened the knot in the handkerchief.

As I stooped, the precious coin fell with a tinkle and rolled smoothly, quickly as a ray of light on its yellow glistening body; down it leaped into the bowels of the sea. With it went my sole hope of travelling beyond the Egyptian coast.

I do not think that I have mourned the loss of any sum more than that gold sovereign. But there you are: I had been put on my mettle again.

Within a few brief days, we were nearing the shores of Egypt. They would, of course, have me leave the boat at Port Said. How in the name of all that is holy was I to get further, into other parts of Arabia – with my last pound gone into the sea?

Now they were lowering the gangway, passports were being examined and the first-class passengers were leaving the boat. Within half an hour, I would find myself in a strange city amongst a strange people.

Time for a further intervention in my life. Presently I saw a burly man, dressed in very grubby overalls, running about as if searching for someone amongst the passengers. He talked to several without much success, so it seemed; then he descended the iron steps to our lower deck. I was standing near the gangway.

'Ha!' he shouted out to me. 'Do ye ken this toon?'

I, of course, pleaded ignorance of Egyptian conditions.

'Ye know enough though,' he spoke in a proper sea bark, 't'use yer eyes and yer tongue. Take this and wire off to my wife in ter-rms as ye see in this paper. Wire in French from the shore. Maybe she can get it at Greenock by sundown – and keep the change for yoursel'.'

I did telegraph the message, asking the sex of the newly-born bairn and directing that the reply be sent by radio to the Chief Engineer, who could not get away from his ship, and whose radio was temporarily out of service.

The change left enough to get to Jerusalem with exactly thirty-four shillings over.

Let me look at Port Said first.

3

The City of Sham Romance

It was at Port Said that the average eastbound European had his first whiff of the Orient. He expected to inhale the East in its full flavour: and immediately on setting foot in it. Port Said saw to it that he was not disappointed. He certainly got what he wanted, but came about as close to reality as an Oriental scene in a vintage Hollywood film.

In a word: Port Said with all its tinsel glamour, was merely the European's idea of the East, staged by acute Levantines.

That is not to say that it could not be exciting to those who knew it. It could, for the simple reason that a large proportion of the rascality of both East and West collected there: as in the joint of a badly-constructed sewer. Although the police had this element pretty well in hand, there was bound to be a fair leakage of crime and scoundrelly practice where so many ruffians were gathered. They swarmed like flies around the honey-pots of the incoming boats which, almost daily, dropped their quota of travellers anxious to glimpse the mysterious East for a few hours.

Many of the millionaires who derived their wealth from the oil-Sheikhs are of Port Saidian origins. In Europe and the Americas, you know them by the fact that they are generally called 'Sheikh' or 'Prince' nowadays, and tend to outnumber the genuine articles.

In the 'native' quarter, for which the tourist and the 'griffin' – the greenhorn – on his way to India invariably made, the panorama of what Wordsworth once called 'the gorgeous East' displayed itself in all the hues which the credulous Occidental believes to be inalienable from it. Bazaars where everything from cheap meerschaums made in East Asia to scented necklaces turned out in Europe, Turkish daggers from Sheffield and Egyptian shawls from Turin were sold.

There were dancing booths, where faded Parisiennes garbed as *houris* wriggled in dances supposed to be 'Eastern'; giving the impression that it takes at least half-a-century's hard work to break into a dancing job. There were cafés, where sleek waiters of an indeterminate kind handed out wicked-looking drinks just as harmless as sherbet; and halls of variety, where sights which would shock Mrs. Grundy to death are supposed to be seen but which are really rather behind the standard of most London theatres in this respect.

The last time I stopped at Port Said was on my way back to Europe from India, not so many years ago. Although air transport has made it largely redundant as a tourist attraction, it was very much the same old Babel as ever. A perfect picture of the doer and the done, the first going about his business with the stale expression of the everyday business man; the latter taking it all in with the *bonhomie* of the credulous Westerner who rather likes to be swindled.

There were, of course, cases where the Westerner cuts

up rough, but these were few: I noticed that, for some reason, complaints usually came from men and women who could scarcely be mistaken for anything other than Londoners. The rest took it as incidental to the voyage.

But the occasion on which I saw most of Port Said was the time when I resolved to spend three days there on returning from a mission to Alexandria.

The blackguardly colony of cosmopolitans rather intrigued me from the comic point of view, and I felt inclined to study its behaviour at closer quarters. There could not but be, I felt, a wealth of the petty picturesque in this, the first street in the world's East End.

So I disguised myself as a somewhat seedy-looking and down-at-heel Turk, with shabby fez and worn frock-coat, and began to compare notes with the local banditti.

The first rascal I encountered – and a tiresome enough one at that – was a gentleman who arranged abductions. He was a down-and-out Irishman who had found himself stranded at Port Said some twenty years before, and who had taken to the place as affording a congenial spot for his natural bias to rascality.

You could scarcely have told him from an Egyptian of the middle class, so faithfully had the environment dealt with him. Indeed, his reddish hair and freckled face were characteristic of a certain type of North Egyptian of Turkish extraction.

A drink or two induced in him a communicative mood, and as he seemed to take me for one of his own kidney, a view I encouraged, I soon had from him the details of his picturesque business. In this, he was assisted by several young women of marked histrionic ability.

His *modus operandi* was as follows: one or other of the little beauties he employed approached the greenest young Englishman or Frenchman they could find and, in affecting broken English or French, spun a pitiful story of a cruel father or an unhappy home.

In about twenty per cent of cases the greenhorns swallowed the bait, and agreed to rescue the entrancing Eastern maiden from the dreadful conditions in which she lived, by affording her an opportunity of escape. In some instances the moon-struck idiots, regarding themselves as the heroes of an Eastern romance, even went so far as to propose elopement.

As a preliminary, the enchantress usually enticed her victim into the garden of the 'Effendi's' house in the native quarter, assuring him that her stern parent was away from home. It was then that the procurer swooped.

That swoop of his was a masterpiece of parental wrath and outraged grief. It usually cost the griffin, who had no wish to cool his heels in an Egyptian calaboose, anything from fifty to a hundred pounds. Not in one single instance, my shady acquaintance assured me, had any application been made to the police. The shock of disillusionment and perhaps the terror of a lost job, were usually powerful incentives to a peaceful solution.

Only in one instance did the old rascal get more than he bargained for. That was in the case of a brother Irishman, many years before, who was on the way to India to take up a post as a junior police-wallah. The punch behind his fellow-countryman's fist, he assured me, as he ruefully rubbed his jaw, would always remain as a reminder of the militant propensities of the race to which they both belonged. It was however, the one liability he had to enter in an otherwise flourishing ledger.

The ancient lady who ran an 'opium-den' was scarcely as communicative; but, when I assured her that I was an inoffensive wayfarer, she entered somewhat into the spirit of the thing, and came across with the details of her rather comical business. The 'opium' she dispensed to the young fools who came to her dive in search of a novel sensation was, she told me, of a strength so absolutely innocuous as not to harm even the most fragile constitution. A strong cup of coffee administered after the 'smoke' invariably cleared the heads of her customers sufficiently to permit them to catch their steamers in plenty of time.

The experience usually cost them a sovereign or thereabouts, and local music and dancing were thrown in. How local the entertainment was, varied according to whether the musicians and dancers were White Russians, Bulgarians, or Romanians.

Probably the dupes were no more the worse for it than if they had taken one over the eight somewhere around Piccadilly.

But, as she was not slow to remind me, they had obtained at a relatively trifling cost, a tale of their familiarity with Eastern dope-dens which would guarantee a respectful hearing for the rest of their lives, especially in the suburbs from which most of them originated.

There were, of course, darker aspects to this bazaar of minor villainy which I do not intend to specify; sordid means of livelihood of the most horrible kinds, but generally speaking, these were designed more for the excitement of the resident population than for the tourist or traveller.

Among the more amusing means by which the note was nimbly charmed from the wallet of the visitor was the gambling den. So far as want of ventilation goes, in these places the mephitic suffix was fully justified.

Careful examination of the roulette wheels in these tawdry pleasure-houses enables me to say that they were usually within the entire control and manipulation of the croupier who, by a quick glance, could see precisely how much was placed upon the various numbers, and could, by controlling a certain number of revolutions of the wheel, so manage things that the index pointed to almost any figure he chose, with very nearly mathematical certainty.

But the dance-halls are, above all, the resorts in which the European and American passing through Port Said found the kind of atmosphere he expected. In the entrance porticoes of these were usually to be seen one or more specimens of those ladies who seek by ventral wrigglings to create the impression that they are engaged in an Oriental *pas seul*.

The majority of these were Frenchwomen of *passé* appearance and tough reputation. They were usually dancers, good enough of their kind, though the contortions in which they indulged bore, as a rule, but little resemblance to Eastern dancing proper.

But the inner mysteries of these places were dedicated to modern dancing and here the traveller might be seen disporting himself with the best imitation of an Eastern *houri* which the place could afford. Young ladies from Armenia, Greece, or the Slavic lands, for the most part, they were plentifully beautified with paint, their eyebrows heavily daubed with kohl. Their nails, both on hands and toes, were scarlet with henna – and they jingled, like the fine lady who rode to Banbury Cross, with sequins, beads and even bells.

Oddly enough, it is in such places that one may often pick up an Egyptian antiquity – I don't mean anything in the female line. A scarab or a piece of 'the original Pharaoh's' sarcophagus (what an extensive coffin it must have been, to be sure), or an amulet from the grave of Osiris.

Though wrongly described, really valuable treasures still often turn up at Port Said.

The Egyptology of the vendors is generally weak; though their English is sometimes amazing: especially when dozens of them claim to be former directors of the Egyptian Museum in Cairo.

But their really strong point is arithmetic, when it comes to counting in foreign currency.

Port Said! The heart of Oriental mystery!

4

Jerusalem

I do not think that I will weary the reader with an account of my long trek up to Jerusalem.

Unlike an ordinary traveller, my time was my own and I was not so much out to see sights and to place a pencilled tick against their names in a previously prepared itinerary, as to fulfil a challenge: to absorb certain atmospheres and manage to survive.

The Oriental and biblical background is still there – will in fact, never be obliterated, but whereas earlier, the foreground had been nothing but unproductive desert, a few grape-growing colonies and terraced slopes where, with infinite labour, fruit and vegetables were induced to grow: it is now occupied by towering edifices of concrete, vast generating stations and, wonder of wonders, even a soap factory.

Soap in Palestine! What an anachronism!

When the Turks advanced on the Suez Canal and dragged with them those heavy pontoons later to be seen, holed and shot-ridden, in the public gardens outside Cairo, they made painful progress. They placed palm branches on the sand, and upon the branches they laid mats.

That roadless time is more years ago than some of us

care to remember; yet the passage of time has been relatively brief – ridiculously so in a country such as the Holy Land, which remained unchanged for many centuries.

When the British armies decided to launch an advance upon the Turkish forces in Palestine, their top brass looked at the yielding sands of the desert, gazed upon the palm-and-branch roads of the slowly retreating Turks, shook their heads sadly and called in the Engineers, as they always do on such occasions.

'We want roads,' said the Gunners (the infantry have no say in such matters, and that is why infantry is always spelt with a small 'i'); the Royal Engineers, baffled, straight away conferred with the Sappers.

Now, one of these Sappers had a wife who insisted upon keeping fowls, and it was the Sapper who had had to make her hen-roost.

Thus it was that wifely determination and man's innate cowardice solved the transport problems of the British armies.

This Sapper had had to wrestle with many yards of chicken-run wire and he had discovered, among other things, that it would bear his weight when placed upon the ground. He secured some, planted it on the desert sand, and invited the Gunners to proceed.

The Gunners found that the wheels of their war-chariots now remained above the level of the sand, and they fell upon the Sapper and blessed him in potations of Alexandrian beer.

The cables hummed and it was discovered that in Australia there were hundreds of miles of chicken-netting. There they used it to keep the rabbits out.

Seven hundred miles of wire-netting were pegged out across the desert of Palestine in World War I, and all who would make progress, from Lord Allenby downwards, had to traverse it.

There was, it is true, a misguided officer who introduced a tank. He brought it in sections to the battle-front, assembled it, and then sent it forward.

Slowly, ignominiously, yet humorously, it churned up the desert, gradually dug a neat hole into which it subsided and proceeded to sleep there for the rest of the War.

I reached Jerusalem by rail from El Kantara on the Suez Canal and the journey was a very comfortable one.

When the R.E.'s first laid the track in the War years as far as Ludd, the reverse was the case.

They had to hurry, and speed meant more than comfort. Consequently, as soon as the rails were delivered from England, they were laid upon the desert, the track being allowed to follow all the contours of the landscape.

Travellers on the railway in those days had both alarming and amusing experiences. The carriage would rock from side to side and dip and oscillate like a dinghy in a rough sea. Drinking out of a cup or a glass was an impossibility because of the violent movements. Travellers quickly found that the only way to convey liquid safely to the mouth was to place the neck of a bottle firmly between the teeth and to suck hard.

The engines – what funny engines they were too! Their funnels had grown stiff and tall with age, and try as they might, they could not altogether shake off the suburban respectability of the siding. They, too, often suffered from the pangs of thirst. Water for them was a very serious matter. Sometimes they drank too much and then they became red-hot. Then the stokers would draw the fires, the passengers would decant upon the desert and there all would lugubriously remain until another stiff-funnelled ancient wheezed perilously into sight.

Now all this was changed. The travel bureau round your nearest corner would sell you a sleeping-car ticket for the El Kantara-Jerusalem journey.

Very little is known about the early days of Jerusalem: but it is obvious that the dominating position which it occupies made an irresistible appeal to the worshippers of Baal.

Around the Temple to Baal a township of sorts grew up, and then it had to be set out for defence. When Solomon was there in all his glory it had become a vast citadel. Walls surrounded it and it was a magnificent capital.

Jerusalem has been a war-centre throughout the ages and although the two World Wars left it unscathed, many of those of the past were waged over it and in it, and the havoc which was wrought was immense.

Yet, notwithstanding these depredations of old, the city is packed with interest. Jerusalem the Golden is no place for a fleeting visit, for here we have a centre where many faiths meet, where Moslem jostles Jew and where the Christian Protestant walks shoulder by shoulder with the Orthodox Greek.

Because of this conglomeration of faiths, it is impossible to say which is the principal of the relics to be found within the city walls. There is the Church of the Holy Sepulchre, to which the ex-Kaiser presented gems subsequently discovered to be imitation. This imposing structure is high above the Via Dolorosa, where inscriptions mark the stations of the Cross. Within the Church is the site of the Cross and a portion of what is declared to be the beam which Christ so laboriously carried; and as the name implies, there is the most sacred of all Christian Shrines, the Holy Sepulchre.

It was Saint Helena, the mother of Constantine the Great, who founded the Church. She travelled extensively and at Jerusalem she is said to have discovered the Tomb and near it the Cross, buried beneath rocks nearby. The rocks bore indentations, shown to her and to all comers ever since, and said to be made by the tears of the Virgin.

Whilst there is no possible doubt regarding the Sepulchre, a considerable difference of opinion exists as to the site of the Crucifixion. The redoubtable General Gordon identified as Golgotha, a knoll outside the Damascus Gate.

The Tomb in the Church of the Holy Sepulchre has, for centuries, been the centre of much strife between the Christian sects – the antagonism being due, of course, to the zeal of the worshippers.

All desired a part in the custody of the Tomb of Christ, and were certainly not prepared to turn the other cheek over the matter. During the Ottoman suzerainty, the Turks were often driven to distraction by the warring of the sects.

Copts, Latins and Orthodox Armenians share the actual shrine but there were more than twenty other denominations who felt that they too, should have a part. Conflict was inevitable in such circumstances and during the days of the Turkish regime, it was found necessary to post a guard of soldiers close to the Tomb to maintain some semblance of peace.

Sacred to all Moslems is the site of Solomon's Temple in the precincts of the Haram-es-Sherif (The Elevated Sanctuary) and upon which the Dome of the Rock now stands.

One enters the Haram-es-Sherif and comes upon a vast paved court with picturesque old buildings on two sides.

Marble columns enclose the central terrace where stands the Dome of the Rock.

The roof and the sides are of beautiful tiles, mellowed green with age, and the interior is adorned with ninth-century mosaics and scrolls upon which are inscribed verses from the Koran.

A railing completely encircles the rock itself. It is deeply fissured with indentations, believed to be marks made by the fingers of the Angel Gabriel.

Quite near – too near for the peace of Jerusalem on past occasions – is the Wailing Wall of the Jews. It is here, beneath Mount Zion, that Jews flock from all parts of the world. On the evening before the Sabbath, they lower their faces against the great wall of the Haram and wail and call upon God to restore to the Chosen People the site of Solomon's Temple.

The Garden of Gethsemane lies beyond the Golden Gate of the Haram-es-Sherif. This gate has been walled up for more than four hundred years. The Garden is on the upper slopes of the Valley of Jehoshaphat. From here paths wind up to the Mount of Olives from the eastern summit of which Christ ascended to Heaven.

This hallowed spot is marked by a small mosque, transformed from a Christian Church built by Constantine in the fourth century.

The simplicity of this shrine, together with the impressive yet pleasing simplicity of the Haram-es-Sherif, is in striking contrast to the modern decoration of the Church of the Holy Sepulchre, and of the Chapel of the Nativity at Bethlehem some five miles from Jerusalem.

The simple manger under the Star of Bethlehem is now in Rome, and its place has been taken by an ornate marble structure within an ornamental grotto. The lighting is provided by fifteen silver lamps, each one of which is tended by a different Christian denomination.

The Altar of the Adoration of the Magi, which marks the spot where the Wise Men knelt when they went to offer gifts to the infant Christ, is still more ornate. All is in marked contrast to the beautiful simplicity of the fourth-century Basilica of Constantine which adjoins.

And now a little more background – still not far from modern Jerusalem. Hebron, known to the Arabs as El Khalil – the City of Abraham, the Friend of God – is midway between Jerusalem and Beersheba.

The story of Hebron is wrapped up with those places found nearby – the Vale of Tears and the Tomb of Abraham.

The Tomb has long been in Moslem keeping and a great mosque is built over it. At the door of the mosque, one is shown the cave where lie buried Abraham and Sarah, their sons and their wives. None has descended into the cave for centuries.

As I have noted, Hebron is still very much the City of Abraham. Groups of Arabs sit around in the shade of the trees and converse gravely. They have little more to do. When the time comes to till the soil or to gather the harvest, they bestir themselves, but not unduly.

There is a premium on masculine energy in Hebron.

And the men still take their time from Abraham, whose tomb they guard. They are often still content to harness a diminutive donkey next to a camel and allow the twain to scratch the earth with a primitive wooden plough, the patent for which was taken out before Abraham espoused Sarah.

Only the women have the itch to work.

Perhaps the men see to it that the irritation is constant.

Besides, the affairs of the City of Abraham have to be discussed. And that is man's work – fatiguing work, necessitating long periods of repose.

Further afield there is the site of Mizpeh, where Samuel judged Israel for twenty years.

On the way to the Jordan and the Sea of Galilee one passes a succession of biblical sites where nothing has been changed. Near the village of Askar there is the Well of Jacob where Christ met the woman of Samaria.

It cannot be long before the water of Jacob's Well is raised by an electric pump with power supplied from the River Jordan!

Then one passes the Tomb of Joseph. This is near Nablus, the capital of Samaria. Once this was a fine city, but when I first saw it, it housed no more than fifteen thousand inhabitants.

A few miles away is a track which leads up to the ruins of the old city of Samaria. The history of this ancient town is a story of one long series of battles dating from the time of Ahab. Then it was one of the centres of the worship of Baal.

Alexander the Great levelled old Samaria to the ground in 331 B.C., and it was rebuilt. Soon however, it was in ruins again. Herod was well-acquainted with Samaria, and it is from his epoch that the present ruins date.

A number of magnificent marble columns, standing amid carved stones, were unearthed there by an expedition from the University of Harvard.

Even modern Nablus had a narrow escape from destruction in 1918, when the victorious troops of Lord Allenby pursued the fleeing Turks.

Assisted by their German Allies, the Turks made many

a brave stand and the British guns thundered perilously close to Nablus.

And then the Turkish horde finally broke and retreated by mountain paths in the direction of old Samaria. Aeroplanes followed them and harried them with machine-gun and bomb and then, when they eventually emerged from the hills, they discovered to their chagrin that Allenby's cavalry had meanwhile worked round the hills and had cut off their retreat.

There was one curious thing attaching to the capture of Nablus which bears telling.

It was noticed that the privates of an Indian regiment, bivouacked under trees, had provided themselves with camp-beds – several scores of them. On inspection, it was noticed that these camp-beds were of English pattern. On a closer inspection it was found that they bore the names of British officers.

It did not take long to clear up the mystery. The beds had belonged to the British officers captured in Kut-el-Amara in Mesopotamia.

The Turkish headquarters had appropriated them and transported the lot for their own use in Palestine. They retained them to the last, until indeed, they were shelled out of them by British guns at Nablus. Spoils of war are nobody's property but those who are strong enough to hold them.

I left the battlefield of Samaria behind and moved on to the Esdrealon Plain. Then I passed on to the Pass of Megiddo, the scene of many another bloody battle, from the time of the Pharaohs to Napoleon.

Then, gradually ascending the hills of Galilee, I came to Nazareth. The interest in Nazareth centres more or less entirely around the story of the youthful Jesus, and of Joseph and Mary. It has never been the scene of any great conflict – a fact which is perhaps explained by its secluded position in the lower hills.

In Nazareth is the Church of the Annunciation. Steps descend to the Chapel of the Annunciation, and a broken column marks the spot where the Angel spoke to Mary.

Here also are the dwelling and the kitchen of the Virgin. Over the workshop of Joseph a chapel has been erected; and over a large stone known as the Table of Christ there is another.

Yet another chapel denotes the spot where Jesus preached in the Synagogue, and the spot from which he was driven by the Nazarenes.

Mary's Fountain (Ain Miriam) is still used by the women of Nazareth much in the same way as it was used by Mary. They congregate there and gossip while waiting for their turn to fill their long earthenware jars, which they carry gracefully away upon one shoulder.

From Nazareth the road goes through country rich in biblical associations. As it rises among the hills one can make out the town of Kefr Kenna, built over land of Galilee, the Mount of Beatitudes and the place where Jesus fed the five thousand. Climb still higher and then, suddenly, there is the Sea of Galilee with the small town of Tiberias nestling on the shore. Capernaum can be seen in the distance where the River Jordan carries its waters into the sea.

Tiberias is famed among two, at least, of the peoples of Palestine. It is rather an uninteresting place in itself, but Jews believe that when the Messiah comes he will rise from the Sea of Galilee, gather together his scattered people at Tiberias and proceed with them in triumph to Safeo, which lies in the shadow of Mount Hermon.

The Arabs refer to the place as Sultan el Baraghit, which, being interpreted, means 'King of the Fleas'. It has to be confessed, one of its residents told me, that the appellation is well-merited.

However, one must not be too critical of Tiberias. It would never win a beauty competition, but it at least looks out upon the blue, rippling waters of the Sea of Galilee.

5

Diplomacy and the Roadmaker

It must not be thought, however, that Tiberias has no other claim to fame. Even in the days of Herod it was noted for its hot springs, which are credited with great curative properties. Herod was a frequent visitor here, and often sampled the waters. Now his place has been taken by fashionable crowds, for a spa, with every modern appointment, has been erected over the springs. To my eyes, however, the interior of the domed bath-house was somewhat uninviting.

As for the Jordan itself, which, after all, it was my purpose to visit, this flows through a wonderfully fertile valley, in which are to be found figs, cultivated and wild olives, palm, sycamore, oleander and, above all, henna.

We associate henna with hair, and we are inclined to imagine that its application to the human head for dyeing purposes is a modern innovation born of the twentieth-century feminine demand for beauty-parlours.

In the Pentateuch – the five Books of Moses – there is the story of the Butler and the Baker. It is possible to refer to some reliefs of the Egyptian Middle Kingdom which depict these high officials performing their functions.

Here we see a butler pouring a comforting drink into the cup of his great lady while she is undergoing the strain of the hairdressing toilet.

There is no reason to disbelieve the suggestion that this lady was having her hair treated with Jordan River henna – the white, fragrant-flowered *kopher*, the camphire mentioned by Solomon, in his Song of Songs.

We Orientals have a great regard for this flower, and have at all times associated it with love and marriage. And we have found many uses for henna. Many of our women use it to dye their finger nails. The men even, do not despise it. They utilise its colouring properties in the improvement of their beards, especially when grey or white.

When in the neighbourhood of the Sea of Galilee and of the Jordan, one should take the opportunity to visit The Place of Burning, near Haifa.

Haifa was once a quiet little retreat nestling in the shadow of Mount Carmel, upon whose summit Elijah met and confounded the prophets of Baal.

A small chapel on an eminence stands out picturesquely. This landmark is still known to the Arabs as El Mahrahkah, or the Place of Burning, where was erected Elijah's altar, onto which the miraculous fire descended from Heaven.

On the Mount, too, is a Monastery of the Carmelite Fathers. Here there is a basilica, which is built over the grotto of the prophet Elias. The flat roof of the monastery provides one of the most magnificent views to be seen anywhere in this land – that is, if one neglects to look in the direction of the teeming Port below.

Ordinarily, to reach the Dead Sea, one starts from Jerusalem. It is by far the easiest way, and I do not recommend travellers to do as I did – which was to travel from village to village, willy-nilly, until one sees the waters of the Sea.

Yet the days I spent upon the journey were not uninteresting, if uneventful.

The guide-book way takes one through the Damascus Gate of Jerusalem and down the white road between the Mount of Olives, beloved of the ex-Kaiser, and the ancient walls of the Temple Area to the Valley of Gethsemane.

Coming direct from modern Jerusalem, it is possible quickly to forget the hammering of the builders and to allow one's mind to become placid and receptive and thus to take in the old-world atmosphere.

The road rises to Bethany; here there are no petrol tanks, no kerosene-tin factories and, if one is careful to keep wells out of this purview, few maltreated kerosene tins turned into buckets.

This most impressive biblical site will impress if only because of the simplicity which it radiates.

Mary and Martha had their home in Bethany and the place is still shown. Looking upon the landscape, one accepts the fact that one is looking upon the actual abode of these good women, without the least suspicion of incredulity. It was here, too, in Bethany, that lived Simon the Leper, and it was in his house that the woman washed the feet of Jesus.

From Bethany the country undulates and becomes barren. Then, a mere hour and a half from Jerusalem for modern travellers, there is the Dead Sea, 1,300 feet below the level of the ocean.

The Dead Sea!

The ancients it was who gave this lugubrious title to this

dark expanse of water, and it was sufficiently well merited to be retained over the centuries.

Always it has been a barren and a dreary spot with but a sprinkling of incredibly poor humans eking out a precarious, fever-stricken existence around its shores.

But the moulding hand of the twentieth century is to be found at work even here. A health resort is in existence, with piers and bathing establishments and modern hotels and restaurants.

I decided to test practically the old adage that it is impossible for a human to sink through the waters of the Dead Sea because of its high relative density.

I found the waters to be extremely buoyant, but with effort it was, of course, possible to submerge. I had had an excellent bathe and, as I scrambled uncomfortably into my clothes, I thought that I had made a discovery. The waters, besides being very buoyant, serve as a violent and potent emetic for the unwary! However, others had been before me, and the discovery is to cause this allegedly Dead Sea itself to suffer the pangs of regurgitation.

Roughly ten miles from the northern end of the Dead Sea is that place to which so many generations of Westerners have been bidden to depart – Jericho.

Why it should have become the practice figuratively to consign to this place, and why it should have held a vogue in this respect only comparable with Timbuktu and Hades, I cannot imagine, for it is by no means an unpleasant place.

Presumably it was selected because it was somewhat difficult of access and the return journey was equally lengthy and fatiguing. However, the modern traveller, if he so wishes, can be in Jericho within a very short time of leaving Jerusalem.

Twentieth-century Jericho is by no means remarkable,

but the orange groves, palm trees and the large variety of flowers in the gardens make it stand out invitingly from the barren surroundings.

As did the old, modern Jericho depends entirely upon the waters of the Elisha's Fountain to make its land fertile. The spring still gushes forth to its beneficent work from the rocky hillside close to the site of the ancient City of Palms.

Little is to be seen of the old city except a few stones of great size, revealed by excavation. It was, however, a place of no small importance in olden times, lying as it did upon the main caravan route. Its basic industry, centred around Elisha's Fountain, was the provision of water.

I had the misfortune, when there, to be visited by an old acquaintance of mine – sand-fly fever – and this incapacitated me for several days. I stayed with a friend and, while recuperating, spent some quite amusing hours gossiping with the locals.

There was one benign and venerable figure who was happiest when giving rein to his remarkable vein of penetrative, yet subtle humour. In much of what he said there lurked a substratum of truth, even though this was invariably embroidered with an intriguing pattern of Eastern fancy.

It was this gentleman, whom I named the Oracle, who told me much of the difficulties of those who had laboured here since the nineteen-twenties.

Particularly beset with difficulties had been the engineers who raised towns and made roads, for they came from the West with plane tables, chains and rulers and proceeded to draw straight lines over ground which had sacred associations for, and therefore caused anxiety to, men and women of various religions.

In gauging the achievements of the engineers here-abouts we are wont to take a material view and to weigh only their accomplishments in terms of steel, concrete and kilowatts. But the engineers have had to be diplomats first and engineers second.

There was the roadmaker whose way was stopped by the possessions of an irascible old landowner who dwelt in the past and spat scornfully at the mere mention of laws.

To him went a subordinate engineer and one who was well versed in the art of Eastern badinage. Unto the old man, did that man of blue-prints unloose the bridle of fancy: or of Eastern experience – who knows?

'Away, over the caravan routes in Iraq,' he said, 'there is a very wise Emir. His possessions are great, but they are greater now than they were, even though they are less.'

The aged one who had been restlessly swaying to and fro and allowing his eyelids to fall in affectation of listlessness and inertia, paused in his movements and eyed the story-teller with unconcealed suspicion.

He pondered heavily and then muttered: 'Greater, yet less! What nonsense is this? Surely this young man of travel and seeming learning has been accursed by Shaitan, for indubitably he is mad.'

Quite unperturbed, the young engineer proceeded in his discourse. 'Yes, verily,' he said, 'this will become manifest during the recital, as do all things in good time. To resume: this wisest of all Emirs, even though he gave, knew that in so doing, he was receiving tenfold.'

'How is this?' demanded the irascible one.

'In many ways,' responded the engineer, 'for he gave land for a road and now all the land that adjoins has more than doubled in value.'

'Fool! Are you suggesting that I shall provide land for the building of one of these roads which bring pestilential motor-cars and undesirable travellers and worry the sheep and scare the she-camels – I, of those who have held on to our land for generation after generation and who am known throughout the countryside as one of those who are not to be beguiled by those who indulge in sharp practices? I should give: who have never even allowed to have taken from me?

'Besides,' he went on somewhat artlessly, 'methinks you stated that this wise Emir was repaid tenfold. And now you tell me that his land merely doubled in value. You lack veracity in your tale-telling, you mere maker of roads.'

'Indeed, I do not,' enthused the engineer, 'for indeed, I understated matters when I said that the Emir received tenfold. Not only has the value of his land increased, but, the people of the countryside, realising the blessings which his wisdom has brought upon them, were loud in their praises.

'So overjoyed were they, that they made up a deputation which besought an audience of him. Respectfully they prayed that they be allowed to approach the authorities with a prayer that the road be named after him. The Emir graciously agreed and now that road bears the name of this great man of unbounded wisdom.

'And that road is one which will last as did those laid down by the Romans, thousands of years ago.

'Therefore, the name of this illustrious man will endure for ever more. The generations which come after him will tell of his wisdom; they will chant his praises and they will revere his name. Yea, even his tomb will be a place of sacred pilgrimage. All this, mark you, O one of magnanimity and discernment, because he, in his wisdom, sold but a tiny portion of his land.'

'What would be required,' asked the old man after

pondering awhile, 'should the people of this countryside decide – ahem, to send a deputation to me, for instance, and ask for land for a road?'

'But very little,' answered the engineer. 'The road could enter your lands at Sidi-Abas and proceed in a straight line to your boundary. Such a straight line without deviations would take the smallest amount of land, for as you know, the shortest space between any two given points is that which is made by the straight line.

'There might, however,' he proceeded, 'be some objections to such a line as it would undoubtedly, here and there, pass over certain houses whose occupants might object.'

'Object!' growled the stout old gentleman, 'Object! Who are they to object? A straight line it shall be and if there are any objections, well, you just send the objectors to me.'

'You will, of course, be compensated for parting with land for the roadway and no doubt those whose dwellings will have to be demolished will look for requital from you. In that event, perhaps an order from you promising to make amends would be requisite.'

'But if I am to give this land on which would be built a magnificent road – so magnificent that the surrounding people will of their own accord demand that it be named after me – what further blessings should they want?' The ancient was adamant.

'Compensation for them! And from me! The very idea is fantastic, young man. But perhaps you did but jest. I note that you require an order from me *promising* compensation. It shall be given. It will matter not. The fulfilment of the order will rest with me. Promising is one thing and happening is another. It will at least let the people rest in hope and make them the readier the more quickly to organise that unanimous committee which shall do honour to my name.'

And so it was that the road was commenced. An army of workmen was recruited and the engineers departed from their straight line not so much as a hair's breadth. True, it was, that many a dwelling had to be demolished, but the ousted occupants were provided with compensation orders bearing the signature of the landowner and all was well. They went to live with relatives, well knowing that justice, compensation and the like could take decades in these parts, if not generations. Life, after all, was like that.

The chief engineer anticipated no further trouble. He was, indeed, contemplating the chances of a favourable answer to an application for leave when work on the road was suddenly stopped.

Those who went on ahead of the workmen, taking levels, estimating materials and generally preparing the way, found that their straight line was to bring them directly upon an ancient and tumble-down mosque. The architect had noted it in passing, but had registered it in his brain merely as an insignificant, unimportant ruin. He had noted it thus because it occupied a site around which, should a detour have to be made, much difficult work and intricate engineering skill would be called for.

Those who did the actual work for him, however, stopped aghast when they saw where their plan was taking them, for what lay in their path was nothing less than the tomb of a venerated bygone dervish. True that few now went to the spot to pray and remember him, but to desecrate such a place by bulldozing it out of existence would be to rouse the instantaneous hatred of all the countryside and, who could say, perhaps a rebellion on a small scale which might even have further very unpleasant repercussions.

Besides, those who normally obeyed the behests of the chief engineer and the subordinate engineer and the other engineers who did most of their work at a large table in a large office, were good Moslems themselves. That is why they stopped work, and stopped immediately.

The disquieting news was conveyed to the chief engineer who, groaning, cast aside those pleasant thoughts of the flesh-pots of home and consulted with his second-in-command.

Immersed in gloom, both battled for hours with fresh plans and specifications. They came to the reluctant conclusion that such was the contour of the land that a deviation from the straight line in the vicinity of the tomb would undo much of the work already accomplished. Worse still, it would render necessary a revision of the estimates and an application to the Powers That Be for a considerable augmentation of funds.

The chief engineer definitely abandoned the idea of an application for leave, but turned his thoughts rather to the probability or otherwise of not losing his job.

Such was the dreariness and barrenness of the situation when the subordinate engineer, a born diplomat as we have seen, had a further brain-wave.

He would, he said, interview the irascible landowner once again and endeavour to develop a way out of the seeming impasse.

To the house of the landowner he repaired. Now he was received as an honoured guest and after a repast wherein newly-killed and consequently very tough mutton with sour sheep-milk, and much full-flavoured rice vied for the principal place on the menu, he was able to express his satisfaction for the hospitality conferred upon him.

In many parts of the East such appreciation of one's enjoyment was expressed by a gentlemanly exhibition of belching and the host anxiously gauged his success as such by the rise and fall in the crescendo of sound.

In this instance, aided by the sour sheep-milk, the subordinate engineer was able to do more than justice to the meal and the aged host beamed with a powerfully satisfied reaction.

In those days, as my friend the raconteur interrupted himself to tell me, it was easier to achieve success in entertaining, because of the stomach-gas-index. 'Today,' he grumbled, 'eructation merely means that you cannot afford bicarbonate of soda. Time marches on.'

It had been an anxious few minutes, for the engineer had thought that he was going to be sick; but he saved more than his reputation when he succeeded in transforming a western abdominal turbulence into an eastern geniality of manners.

It is less than generally appreciated, however, that in such ways, contributory and essential prerequisites of many great engineering feats are accomplished.

Basking in the mellow and kindly disposition of his host, the subordinate engineer seized his opportunity.

'O man of wisdom,' he said, 'as you will universally be styled when this great and wondrous road is completed, I have given many nights to the contemplation of your fertility of mind and the reverence which is in your heart for your forbears and all that has gone before.

'There is no man such as you, in the whole of this vast countryside, who has done more to uphold the traditions of his race and the fair name of his noble family.'

The roadmaker paused for breath to observe the effect of his words; but, except for a more than ordinarily potent belch, the old man gave no sign. His eyes, however, were crinkled like a vulture's.

The engineer judged it time to pause and apply the stimulus of silence.

'The road,' the host was at length constrained to say, 'how is it progressing?'

'Oh, the road? Magnificently,' responded the engineer with an enthusiastic smile. 'It will be a great monument to your forethought for your people and your countrymen and, of course, to your amazing business acumen.

'As you indicated when, in your wisdom, you first conceived the idea of this road, it proceeds in a line that is absolutely straight. It points like an arrow to the fertility of the mind of him who will rightly confer upon it the great honour of his illustrious name. Future generations shall say: Here is that which was conceived by a noble man – a holy man – a man who dazed his own generation by the scintillation of his own brilliance.'

'Noble words, young man,' acquiesced the old man, with animation. 'It is but right that the fruit of my powerful intellectual labours should be so appreciated, and that it should be a straight road is right, too. The road, posterity will acclaim, is as straight as were my dealings with my fellow men.'

'Yes,' broke in the engineer, 'and when they recount the great difficulties that beset you, they shall applaud your name the more.'

'Difficulties, difficulties?' responded the landowner. 'Indeed, the difficulties were great. I have had to part with much land. And for a pittance, as you know.'

'And there is the matter of your tomb, yet to be erected.'

'My tomb, young man? Do you think that I am about to die? Am I not to see the completion of the road?'

'The association of individual death with the tomb is, essentially, insignificant,' the younger man rejoined. 'True, the tomb is a receptacle for the human clay, but that is as nothing compared with the name which it com-memorates – especially if that name be an illustrious one.'

'But what has my tomb to do with the road?' the now wide-awake host asked suspiciously.

'Posterity will say that it was the shining pinnacle of your many wonderful achievements,' artlessly suggested his companion.

'Along the road that is to be straight is a mosque where, forgotten by those who should do him honour, lie the remains of a bygone saint.'

'One would assume that, left as he is in such absolute abandon, the spirit of this holy man would be at peace, yet it is not so. Missing for many generations have been the prayers of the Faithful and the spirit of the holy man, according to universal report, is restless.'

'But,' interposed the landowner, 'who would trouble to go to that woebegone place to utter their prayers? It has not been done within living memory.'

'That is so,' agreed the other, 'and I think that you will agree with me when I suggest that that is all the more reason why the spirit of this great saint should be at last composed.'

'I am certain,' he added after a significant pause, 'that when you rehearse in your night-thoughts the customary review of the day's doings and omissions, that the germ of this shining achievement will be made plain to you.'

'It may be that you will have a visitation and that it will be suggested to you that dignity could once more be restored to the name of this enormously pious, world-renowned saint, if you erected a mosque in that beautifully shady portion of your garden and had his bones restored thither.'

'It could be so arranged that, as the earthly benefactor of this holy man, you, on your demise, could share his mausoleum and shed the lustre of your presence upon his memory.'

'And there is no doubt,' hastily resumed the engineer as he saw the other struggling for words, 'that, were you to transport the saint to a place of befitting dignity, many pilgrims would pause on their journey and leave offerings large and small, for the poor.'

The landowner, deep in thought, resumed his petulant swaying, so characteristic of the man.

The engineer, for his part, watched his host narrowly, feeling that though his tale had been told, and well told, yet the result still lay in the lap of the gods.

Eventually the old man spoke.

'As you have doubtless heard on all sides, I have long cogitated,' he said, 'over the conditions of the tomb and of the unseemliness of the surroundings for the mortal clay of so great a saint. You may not realise that, although a local man, this saint was known throughout the world.' He took a gulp of smoke from his water-pipe.

'Without doubt, it would be shedding added lustre upon the memory of this holy man were I to erect, in that beautiful corner of the garden, a shrine of elegance to which the remains could be removed. Unquestionably, also, it would be well if I lay there when, in the years to come, I cease to take my benevolent interest in this earth.'

'I will hold communion in the night watches and maybe I shall have a visitation.'

'And the offerings to the – ahem – poor – they may be considerable. I would, of course, be the trustee during my lifetime, the sole trustee.'

'Now I think that blue Damascus tiles would be best for the dome; but, as I say, I must take counsel in the watches of the night. It is remarkable how you share my own thoughts in this matter.'

The road is now built. It is straight. It bears the illustrious name of the landowner whose land has been multiplied in value; cars and buses now run upon its surface and the inhabitants of the district find it easy to transport their produce to the markets of the towns. All is peaceful and relatively prosperous.

There is, however, an engineer who knows the truth. The road and all that it has entailed was not brought into existence by the imagination of the planners, labourers, the skill of the draughtsmen or of those products of the universities who directed their endeavours.

Another kind of specialist: and the votive offerings of pious pilgrims were fully as responsible.

6

An Eye for an I.O.U.

After I had recovered from my bout of fever, I made preparations to continue my journey eastward into the desert of Jordan. It was on Allenby's Bridge – an imposing structure of iron and stone thrown over the River Jordan – that I met an old friend, a British Colonel, whose car had broken down. He joined me on my journey to the capital.

We followed the winding road up to Es Salt. It was a veritable paradise of flowers; seldom have I beheld such a rich profusion of colour.

There were wild roses, orchids, balsam, gladioli, and many other kinds of flowering plants which I was unable to identify. And they grew wild amongst the rocks, behind grey-blue giant boulders of stone. They grew in bunches, in stray patches everywhere.

Es Salt is a sort of half-way house, a pleasant enough halting-place for travellers on their way to Amman, where the monarch of the Arab State awaited us with true Oriental hospitality.

As both my British companion and I were in a hurry to proceed, we decided not to stay the night at Es Salt, but just to break our journey for brief refreshment.

Several sheikhs of the village did all they could to provide such small items of rations as we wanted, bidding us to stay the night with them. One even asserted that the road was none too safe those days, especially if our car broke down: and the nights were very dark.

The Colonel was sipping his tea, and I was gnawing at the leg of a roasted chicken supplied by our hosts when, in the throng which had gathered to look at the two afflicted of Allah who travelled merely for the love of travelling, I espied a rather odd-looking Bedouin. He had blue eyes – not an impossibility in that area, of course – and he was staring hard at my British friend. And then the face was gone: almost as quickly as I had moved my eyes to pick up another piece of meat.

'Do you know anybody in this village?' I later asked the Colonel, becoming aware of the strangeness of the question, as we swerved past the gate of a caravanserai and the vehicle gathered speed.

'No, of course I do not know anyone in Es Salt,' replied the Colonel almost reproachfully, 'nor do I like this beastly, god-forsaken part of Arabia!' And he let drop his monocle on its black moiré ribbon as he looked at me like an affronted crane.

Taking this to mean that that topic was finished, so far as he was concerned, I engaged him in talk about his wartime experiences.

But he was listless. Every now and then he reminded the driver that we intended to reach Amman by sundown, and that the man should not go to sleep at the wheel. That something was about to happen, somehow, I could not get out of my mind. The sixth sense of the Oriental perhaps also told the driver that something was awry. He constantly looked at the officer and almost snarled. Equally possible was the fact that most Arabs, unaccustomed to obeying foreigners, do not take kindly to being shouted at by British ex-colonels, and the driver was only running true to form.

I was thinking that another short burst of speed would bring us out of the rocky defiles, and Amman should be well within sight. But something within me kept on asking whether we were really going to reach our destination by nightfall!

Whether this feeling affected the Colonel, I did not know; but gradually we drifted into silence whilst the car bumped along on the stony road. Mountain rocks rose spur upon spur, barring the living world with every bend that we negotiated.

A shot rang out, then another bullet spat past; and a third. There was a hissing noise; and we knew that a front tyre of the car had been punctured by the bullet of some concealed enemy.

The bedouin driver was perhaps the bravest of the three of us: certainly he gathered his wits quickest. He called out to the sniper that we were the Emir's guests.

Then the Colonel handed him his revolver and he clambered up the rocks. Presently he was out of sight. A few minutes later we heard an exchange of shots, and then there was only a long, long silence.

The Colonel and I decided to stay where we were, until a passing lorry could give us a lift. But who would pass at such a late hour? Everyone we had met was against travelling by night. We must wait there till the dawn, at any rate. And then darkness fell; suddenly, like a curtain.

'Great Scott!' cried the Colonel, as we heard a whip-crack echo following a close buzzing whizz. 'If that was not a bullet again, what was it?'

'Well, it wasn't a peppermint drop,' I replied, 'and it's left a very clean hole in the canvas of the hood – the kind of hole a musket bullet leaves.'

'I knew your district was bad,' growled the Colonel as he felt for his second revolver; 'but I didn't think that it was as deuced bad as this.' I supposed that he was reverting mentally to his colonial days, and I was the local District Officer . . . Or had he been at that hip-flask of his again?

Another shot followed, its lead nose drilling in and whizzing through a mudguard.

'I think I know who was behind that shot.' I volunteered the information on the strength of a rumour that I had heard in the souks of Jerusalem. 'It's sure to be Ahmed the Black, who, by the way, is not black at all, but an Englishman, and a Londoner at that. Society creep, I believe, who had to get out in a hurry for some problem or other.'

'Yes, for somebody else's problem!' grated a voice at the quarter-light, while a tough face behind a very large revolver peered in at us.

I could now see by the light of my torch that it appeared indeed to be none other than Ahmed, as the elder school of novelists would have said. And the face was that of the curious Bedouin I had seen at Es Salt.

'Well, I'm damned!' said the Colonel, 'if it isn't Seymour!' His booze-red face had managed somehow to go as white as chalk, and the monocle dropped from his staring blue eye. He dropped his gun, which fell to the floor of the car. He scrabbled but could not find it.

'Stupid of you, Curtis, isn't it?' said the interloper, 'running about these stark hills with only a single companion to cover your back. It's four years now since that little game of poker, when you and the rest made a black sheep of me and forced me out of the circle.

'But, thinking over things, sizing them up so to speak, out in these wilds, I think that there was more in that

An Eye for an I.O.U.

business than met the eye. None of our hands were exactly
clean. But you could play the hypocrite better than I
could.'

'I refuse to bandy words with – a robber,' grated Curtis.
'In any case, I do not know what the Hell you are referring
to.'

'That sounds good, doesn't it?' jeered Ahmed. 'Scarcely
logical, and all that sort of thing. Let me remind you here
and now that at the moment you aren't Colonel the
Honourable Algernon Curtis, District Commissioner,
etc., etc., but merely a very scared greenhorn! And you've
reason to be scared, old son, for unless I make a very
extensive mistake you're going to have a skinful of lead
within the next ten minutes.'

'Now look here, Ahmed,' I said, taking a hand in the
conversation, 'I don't know the rights of this little personal matter, but I really can't have you shooting up
colonels in this little patch of Arabia.'

'You keep out of this!' Ahmed snarled, 'this is a private
row between – gentlemen, shall we say? At least, there's a
good margin of doubt as to which was the bigger bastard of
the two.

'Now, Algy, if you're ready, we'll just off into the night
and see who can pot the other. Are you game?'

The Honourable Algernon (although that is not his real
name) tried to bluster. 'I simply don't recognise you,' he
bawled. 'Do you think I am here to exchange shots with
any blasted sneak-thief . . .?'

The moon had now crept above the crags.

'That'll be enough of that.' There was an ugly twist to
Ahmed's face. 'Humph yourself in those swagger Jermyn
Street boots of yours and get up and fight like a man.
You remember . . . well, I won't mention the lady's name
in a place like this,' Ahmed's face grew crueller at the

81

recollection, 'but we both lost her over that little rumpus, didn't we? Well, I've good reason to believe she looks kindly upon me still, but I swore I wouldn't go back to her till I had the privilege of wiping my boots on your dirty hide, you little imitation soldier. Have I got to kick you before you'll get up?'

The Honourable Algernon rose, spluttering.

'You swine,' he gasped, 'I'll have your life for this, damn me if I don't! Insulting the Army, you sod! Lend me your gun,' he said to me, 'I'm going to shoot a pi-dog.'

'Well, since you're both so keen,' I remarked, 'I'll just have to let you have your own way. There's my shooter, and if I have to regretfully report the all-too-sudden demise of a handsome District Commissioner, or the wiping-out of a five-star brigand, don't let the dirty water land on my doorstep. Might I suggest, however, that it would be better if the rough-and-tumble was held over till daybreak?'

But to this neither exalted gentleman would agree. It seemed to be a needle-match with a very ugly memory behind it.

Seizing revolvers, they rushed into the now-moonlit pass, and next minute I saw the Honourable Algy's gun spit fire.

'Damn you, you fool!' I cried. 'Remember you've only got six shots and there's probably seven or eight in his magazine. He'll have you on the last, you cuckoo!'

There was a heavy groan from Ahmed.

I knew that groan. There was the whole of.fiction and the stage behind it, and a chuckle at the end of it, but Algy evidently took it for the real thing, and crowed like a bantam cock in triumph. The next minute he yelled like a scalded cat, as a bullet clipped him in just the place where ladies wear earrings.

'Ouch! my ear!' he yelped. Then: 'Shamming dead, are you?' as Ahmed rolled along the ground. To hit a revolving man in that kind of semi-darkness is, as anyone with experience of a rough-and-tumble or two is aware, among the more difficult things in life.

'Blast you,' howled the Mayfair Colonel, as a second bullet caught the toe of his boot. 'Fight fair, can't you, you lousy brigand?'

'Get down on the sand, you stupid oaf,' I shouted, 'or you'll never see breakfast-time. Down, blast you!'

Algy obeyed with that wonderful sense of discipline inculcated in the best public schools; but he didn't improve matters by writhing about in his new recumbent position.

From the blackness beyond came another vicious spurt of flame. The bullet seemed to pass just over the top of his head. Its message seemed to annoy the District Commissioner considerably.

'Here, I say, you,' he sang out, 'I'm not an Aunt Sally, you know.' Ahmed was shooting off his corners. It was the refinement of vindictiveness.

I felt I must help to wrap things up. 'What a pother about a game of cards and a lady,' I sniggered; and, as if I had pulled the strings, both figures rose and blazed at each other furiously. Their wrists must have shaken, for neither registered a hit.

They had now come very close, both to me and each other: and, throwing down their guns, they rushed at each other like a couple of bull-terriers.

Algy was the heavier of the two, and almost at once he got in a nasty left, which floored the bandit. But Ahmed was immediately on his feet again, wiring into his antagonist. There wasn't much science displayed, but they fully made up for it in ferocity.

Suddenly a scream, such as I don't want to hear again in a hurry, rose out of the pass, and Algy came crashing down, holding his hand to his right eye, or rather to where the eyeball had been.

'Here endeth the first lesson,' laughed Ahmed. 'You'll have to wear a blue eyeglass now, my friend, and mount a phoney optic as well, I fear. Let's call it an eye for an I.O.U., shall we?'

'Go away,' shrieked Algy, no longer the gallant war-hero, 'you beastly maimer.'

'That isn't what you called yourself when you maimed my character,' jeered the bandit, 'but somehow I don't think Polly will like you now, with one peeper and a wobble in your right great toe. You'll probably retire from your lucrative but spurious advisership to woggish mon-archs, and rusticate in Great Missenden for the rest of your yellow existence, you dirty little creep, you rotten card-sharping parasite.'

I heard the galloping of hooves and the galloping of Algy's language, as I dragged him back to the crippled car. What he had actually done to Ahmed in the past I could not worm out of him, but which, I wondered, would have the harder row to hoe? The spoilt beauty-man or the brigand picking up a desperate living among the Arabs of this No-Man's Land?

The worst of these English Society people, it seems to me, is that their feuds are just a little more desperate than any of those in which my own countrymen indulge. Prob-ably they put the whole blame upon the influence of the wild hill-land. But on that memorable evening I couldn't see much to choose in the way of pure savagery between that pair of Society lights and a couple of Middle Eastern peasants who had it in for each other over the theft of a goat.

Thank goodness, we Afghans don't play cards!

In the morning the driver returned safe and sound, having sensibly slept in an adjoining Bedouin encampment. He repaired the car, and was put under oath of secrecy not to mention a word of our adventure to anyone: in Amman or elsewhere, for the Colonel's honour was involved.

At last, the next day, we reached the Emir's capital. The Colonel wore a patch over his eye, and allowed no doctor to treat him, having 'only caught a chill in it'. It was no business of mine to relate the escapade to anyone in Arabia, and I saw no more of him until the other day in Piccadilly.

Between Es Salt and the capital of Jordan there were but few villages, for this range of country was given over almost entirely to the tent-dwellers and their immense flocks of sheep: the Bedouins of Jordan despise him who lives behind bricks and mortar.

Even the Emir Abdullah, installed upon his throne by the British and brought from Mecca for the purpose, found it extremely irksome to be away from the tents. He was a true nomad chieftain at heart, and typical of the people over whom he ruled – a real lover of the desert, and by choice, in more or less constant movement.

The Emir, it is true, had caused to be built an imposing house on the outskirts of Amman, but those who called upon him there were fortunate if they found him at home. More often than not he had slipped unobtrusively away, to sojourn in his tent out in the desert.

The Arab, especially the Arab of this area, has little of civic sense. He has none of that pride which the Englishman has in London; and none of that which the American has for his small town.

It would not greatly perturb him if the capital of his country was constituted in a shifting encampment. This partly explained why Amman was such a small and such an insignificant town. And it is called a city because it is the capital.

Until relatively recently, even its main street was unpaved. For many years after independence, with the exception of the Emir's house, all that it could boast was one street of shops, one or two not very imposing mosques and a straggling array of one-storied houses.

Yet Amman is the ancient Rabbah Ammon: and for thousands of years it was a place of great importance on the caravan routes from southern Syria and Egypt and from the east to Arabia.

Under Alexander the Great it was a large Greek settlement, and, in the third century B.C., it was one of the cities of the Decapolis.

Many remains of this ancient grandeur are still to be seen. On an adjacent hill there are parts of the wall of the citadel; there is a Roman temple and much of a great theatre. Several of the fifty columns which were part of this structure are still standing.

Some day, perhaps, Amman may be restored to its former glory.

So firmly implanted however, is the nomadic spirit in the Arab mind that many people feel that nothing short of generations of stern discipline and confinement to fixed areas could eradicate it. Few administrations would care to bring about such regulations and I doubt very much if one exists which could bring them effectively into force.

On the other hand, the effects of some industrialisation, education and oil-royalties have started a process in the

Arab World, and this, indeed, may be the catalyst that is needed.

From the valley of Amman, great plains extend in the direction of Damascus. Once these lands were fertile and supported a great population. Today little grows but grass and scrub over which the nomad grazes his sheep and camels.

There is no question but that these plains could be made fertile once again and that grain and cotton could be grown in abundance, but it could be at the cost of terrible feuds with the tent-dwellers, who regard a plough with almost as much abhorrence as they do bricks and mortar.

The Arab, over the centuries, has assumed very strong grazing rights and rights to the well-waters. These have been accepted as customary law. One section recognises the rights of another to certain areas and to the grazing and the water to be found there. These rights are regarded as inviolable and for any power to interfere with them for the purpose of introducing a plough would be to court trouble of the most serious kind.

Yet this was not always so. Jordan once had a magnificent system of irrigation and the ruins of many of the old aqueducts can still be seen. And the people of Jordan were not always tent-dwellers. The ruins of many great cities are to be found dotted all over the country, providing a mine of wealth for the historian and the archaeologist.

As one goes northwards, it is more and more evident how firm is the grip of the nomad upon this once wealthy and flourishing country. It is entirely given over to the camel and the sheep, beyond which the nomadic Arab has few interests in this life.

Beyond the confines of Amman, one can travel comfortably on a camel; and this method I chose thenceforth as I journeyed into the almost uncharted regions of north-eastern Jordan. Here, again, is a No-Man's Land to which the Saudis, Iraq, and even the Syrians, have laid claims: though of what merit I cannot say.

But in the desert it is not easy to erect a frontier wall. And here it is that much of the romance of real Arabia dwells.

Its encampments are pitched in the open and free air of the limitless sands, where alone you can feel the real freedom of life. Where there is a small village at the crossing point of trade-routes – for which I was making – there are caravanserais which even now bespeak the traditional glory of Arabia – an Arabia whose religions have exchanged their solid paganism for the very different splendour of the Persia or Rome of old.

7

Perils of Man-Smuggling

As I bent down to unstrap my camel load, someone tugged at the hem of my long, flowing robe. Then the wet nose of the camel touched my bared arm, and I thought that the tail of my loose shirt must have been caught under the bag which I had unloaded. Once again I felt – yes, this time it was certain: a pull at my clothes.

'In the Name of Allah! In the Name of Almighty God!' and the voice of a prostrate form, gurgling from a hoarse throat, was drowned by the sound of the bubbling camels in the quadrangle of our desert rest-house.

With more than ordinary curiosity, I bent down towards the one who had pulled at my garments, and whose words of supplication had been almost swallowed up in the general din of shouting drivers as they unloaded their beasts of burden.

I flashed my torch at the man. He lay, face downwards now: holding his side, apparently in great pain. His eyes – Oh those eyes! I can't forget them – they had a haunted look. And his face – well, you have heard of the fantastic hawklike features of the desert Sheikh? He could have beaten most, if not all, of his film counterparts, for the aristocracy of the desert was writ large on his visage.

Now a change seemed to come over him, as if he was

summoning his last reserves of strength for some action . . .

Suddenly, he leaped up like a wounded panther and snatched the flashlight from my hand.

'Thinkest thou that in the heart of the desert people will spare thy life if they see thee making light without a fire?'

A long memory came back to me, for had I not been shot at, once, in a Bedouin encampment as a magician for 'making light out of nothing, like the one cast down from Allah's Palace'.

The man now squatted down beside me. Our backs rested against my sitting camel. From his cummerbund he produced a paper, shading the light of the torch with the skirt of his long robe whilst I read the epistle.

It was a letter from one of my oldest friends in these parts, begging help for this hunted man!

'Peace be to thee, my brother!' I shook him by the hand, 'What a great honour has fallen upon me. It shall, indeed, be my pride to escort thee, the friend of Murad; for Murad once saved mine life's blood.' – 'Sh-hhh' – he placed his hand on my lips.

I took the tip, for the camel may not understand a conversation, but Allah only can tell who hides behind the camel: and although my new friend knew that I, as Murad's seasoned commercial agent, could smuggle him even to heaven: yet even here and now, he said there were eighteen men in the rest-house who would almost literally drink his blood.

With what care I could bestow, the Sheikh's wounds were attended to by me. His enemies had only half-buried the point of their blades in his thigh, and he had slain three before he got to where I was unloading my mount.

It is true that as trading goes in Arabia, I was not an ordinary merchant, but the roving commission given me by Murad, the merchant prince of Damascus, had made it possible for me to travel safely for many months into the most covetously guarded parts of inner Arabia where inter-clan fighting is so dangerous that they shoot first and ask later. But, indebted though I was to Murad, I would have hesitated a little before agreeing to smuggle his friend to safety had I known then what I was to learn of the facts of the case.

That night I had intended to rest before taking the long sandy stretch that lay before me from the banks of the River Jordan eastwards. But Murad's letter and the plight of the young Sheikh compelled my departure.

A haze floated over the distant sand dunes, as the silvery moon, like a blazing scimitar, rose higher and higher above the horizon. The sleepy gate-keeper rubbed his eyes as my camel lumbered out.

'Thou goest at an evil hour!' he shouted, 'for, beyond the ridge, thy life will be in the palm of thy hand!'

It was fortunate, however, that he did not plunge his spear into the sack that hung by the side of my camel. For a good reason I had accommodated the wounded Sheikh in it; and, stuffing hay in another sack, I had placed it at my back to look like someone sitting behind me.

For three hours my speedy camel did gallop. She was the best trotter in Murad's stables, and the Sheikh felt fairly safe, because not until dawn could any man fire on us during those days of the month of fasting, when all the faithful must remain peaceful to one another during the hours of night.

Then the face of the moon began to tarnish and the sand now showed curious strands of colour in that half-light which betokens the approaching dawn. Then a streak shot up, all along the rim of the desert: the Sheikh wriggled in his suspended cradle, but lay still again when I announced the approaching light of day.

With a sense which comes to desert travellers, the Sheikh and I had a presentiment that we were being followed at a discreet distance. Only of the aircraft or armoured cars searching for the fugitive Sheikh did we have fear.

These were the times of the French Mandate over Syria, and the Sheikh was what today would be called a freedom-fighter.

But maybe the French will spare him, I thought; and have just placed a price on his head only to set the Bedouins of the desert on his trail.

If that were the case, I thought, then we were more than a match for the Bedouins. A smuggled machine-gun provided by Murad, and which equalled the balance of my camel's load, would see to that.

Just as I was rounding the bend of Bin Khiza, I could have yelled with delight at the sight of the tent-dwellers not too far below where French territory ceased. But it was still a good three miles. Hard hoofs hit on rock; presently an Arab climbed up the ridge on our right and then ducked down. We were spotted.

Almost immediately, a bullet sang past me. There was no time to lose. The Sheikh crouched behind a boulder, and in a trice I saw the sack which rode behind me rent to bits by bullets. I was now manning my machine-gun. Knowing that they would not shoot down the camel, I let her run towards the friendly encampments.

Our attackers were spread out fanwise, skirmishing fashion. But our superior arms were playing havoc with their ranks. Muffled faces jumped up and fell before the flailing of the machine-gun fire. Presently their leader steeled himself and stood up with a long-barrelled musket and took aim in the most heroic but foolhardy manner imaginable. A shot from the Sheikh's rifle made him whirl in a frenzied circle, and he dropped on his face.

Now they were closing upon us, now retreating. The automatic weapon barked unceasingly. Then it jammed, as these devil's contraptions seem to love to do.

I appealed to even my game leg to do its best, as I scrambled down, yard by yard, towards the land of friendly Bin Khiza. It was, after all, the nephew of the Sheikh of that tribe who was with me, blazing away for his life. As such he had been introduced in the letter which he had taken from his girdle.

Another attack was launched against us; amazingly, the machine-gun unjammed itself and this attack, too, was repelled. We were crawling to safety as we turned and fired, again and again. Forms of our enemies rose only to be mown down by the devil's own weapon.

Then the burring and whirring sound of aero-engines struck upon our ears. 'What in the Name of Allah . . . !' I shouted.

They swept down; one could see clearly from their wing insignia that they were the French desert patrol. Within a few moments they had landed a small, armed group. But by then we were already arriving at the outpost of Bin Khiza's tents. Free men, in the territory of the free, in Independent Arabia.

A dozen horsemen, led by the Sheikh of the tribe himself, rode towards us, firing a welcoming salute into the air. The leader embraced me with a mighty bear-hug.

News had reached him, by relay courier, mounted on the country's fastest mares, that Murad was having the Sheikh's nephew escorted to him, it was hoped, by me. He anticipated trouble, but not a pitched battle like the one that we had just been through.

'And let mine eyes that have dimmed with waiting alight upon my dearest nephew's lustrous features!' He pulled the cloak from my ward's face.

A murderous gleam stole into the old man's eyes, as he started back from the sight. The one whom I had smuggled made a wry face.

'Aman – Aman – in the Name of Allah I seek peace, and sanctuary!' he said.

'In His Name I give it' stammered the Sheikh.

Then the stranger spoke, in perfect Arabic: 'Aye, it is true that thy nephew wanted to escape, and he confided in me. Him I had drugged and dressed him with mine own uniform, stole his papers and in his guise I have reached safely here out of the hands of my regiment. As to me, my name is Krutz,' and the German renegade hung his head in shame.

I saw the Arab chieftain's thumb curl over the hammer of the carbine. Then he tarried.

'In the Name of Allah thou hast asked peace and sanctuary,' he said, red mounting to his cheeks: 'In His Name I have given it; but go thee back to thy regiment before sundown, for let infidel kill infidel; I shall not pollute my blade by slaying dogs.'

The deserter's eyes shot with blood.

'I shall not go back to the hell from which I have escaped,' he shouted; and as the old Sheikh turned, there was a sharp report. Smoke floated from the mouth of the deserter. In his teeth was the end of the barrel of his rifle. So that, if your way should lie one day to the Wadi of Bin Khiza, see a rudely erected tombstone with 'Al Almani ...' (the German ...) on it.

One lesson which the incident has left with me is that of one thing you can be absolutely sure in desert travel; it is that you can be sure of nothing, least of all your fellow travellers.

I lost my way more than once over the devious tracks of the desert when I trekked back to the south, and I discovered to my amazement, that the Arabs of Jordan have hardly any sense of direction outside the area over which they graze their animals.

Fortunately for me, twenty miles to the east of Deraa is Bosrah, a great conical peak which projects prominently from the hills in the background. This landmark proved essential in my final journeyings in Jordan and it allowed me more than once to correct the failings of so-called Arab guides whom I sometimes recruited from encampments.

If weak in geography, they were always strong in encouragement. Whenever asked where anywhere was, they invariably answered, 'Qarib – it is near!'

Beyond Deraa, one moves into the country of the Druses – a race about whom not a great deal is known and who had a bad reputation with the French for their warlike proclivities, as well as for insisting also that they are originally French and good Catholics. The French constantly complained that the Turks said that, during the days of the Ottoman Empire, the Druses had always sworn they were Turks by origin and good Sunni Moslems.

Personally, however, I found the Druses to be quite pleasant people and not sparing in their hospitality.

The men, especially, are of magnificent physique and they are great horsemen. They have, however, one curious practice: they blacken all around their eyes. I discovered that this was not out of any desire to adorn the manly face. The substance which is used for this treatment is held to keep away the flies – of which there are positive clouds in some areas – and to safeguard the eyes from the glare of the blazing sun.

The men certainly have magnificent eyesight, rivalling in this respect the tribesmen of the Pashtun lands in Central Asia. They can observe even the slightest movement over incredible distances and they are natural and splendid shots.

Life in the Druse mountains can be exciting for the unaccompanied wayfarer, for the tracks over the mountains are littered with boulders which have been precipitated down from above.

Journeying along these paths, every now and again one hears an ominous rumble and looks up at the hillside with no little apprehension. Quite often, miniature landslides obliterate the tracks and bring down with them, rocks and boulders which fly at unexpected angles. Many of these boulders would be sufficient to crush a man or a mule.

I had several narrow escapes from this kind of unpleasant death, but these were the only occasions when I suffered perturbation. The Druses, as far as I was concerned, belied their generally fierce reputation and I found them almost shy, rather than an aggressive people.

All the time, however, one could sense a certain atmosphere. Here were a people who would remain quiet and law-abiding if they were left to their own devices. Quite obviously, they were resentful of intrusion and suspicious of any interference from an outside power.

The Turks, during their regime, evidently realised this. In any case, their suzerainty was quite nominal.

One thing that makes the Druses a rather difficult people to make conform to modern ideas of administration is the nature of their religion. Its secrets are zealously guarded and no man is initiated into the mystic rites until he has more than reached the age of discretion. And when he is admitted into his church, he has to make the most terrible and binding vows never to disclose to any who is not a full initiate, any of the secrets of his faith.

Consequently, the Druses never speak of their religion and little is known about it beyond the fact that it resembles a somewhat curious mixture of Christianity and Islam, and uses secret signs and passwords.

They have one outstanding belief and that is in regard to transmigration. They believe that, at the time of death, the soul passes into whatever is born on their land at that moment – no matter whether the new-born one is human or an animal. Should death take place at a moment when no living thing is born, then they believe that the soul passes away to China; and the people of the Jebel Druse believe that there are many of their race in China.

These people do not worship in churches, mosques or temples, as do those who have other faiths. They are careful to perform their religious ceremonies in some chamber carefully hidden away from the eyes of the curious.

Most carefully guarded also is their sacred book upon which, they say, nobody who has not been initiated with the full rites of the faith has ever been allowed to gaze.

This secrecy which attends the religious observances of the Druses also extends, in some measure, to their relations with people of other races. Many of the troubles of the past have undoubtedly been due to a disregard of this trait.

Farther on northward, when working toward the Iraqian frontier with the Jebel (mountain) Druses left behind, I had the misfortune one night to stay in a small house where a man became sick. Apparently he was taken seriously ill in the middle of the night, for my sleep was disturbed by the shuffling of many feet.

Those who have been taught to respect the sickroom and to enter it only when bidden or by permission of the doctor, would view with amazement that which transpires in this part of the Near East when a man is unfortunate enough to be ill.

The noise in this house was such that sleep was impossible. When I rose to investigate the cause of the confusion I found the place filled with friends and curious neighbours who had been hastily summoned to render aid. This motley crowd was busily engaged in prescribing all manner of incredible remedies and charms, mostly at the tops of their voices.

The man's bed, a hard pallet on the floor, was literally surrounded by those anxious to try their medical skill. It was quite obvious that the patient was seriously ill, for already two freshly-killed chickens had been applied warm to his feet.

Every few minutes the unfortunate was dosed with an evil-smelling concoction, declared, by the old lady who had apparently dispensed it, to be capable of restoring any but one who was actually dead.

It was in my heart to believe her, too. I should have had to have been on the verge of coma not to have arisen and hurriedly fled from that noxious smell.

Others who assisted, plied the patient with charms made of earth, and yet others were deliberating whether or not one should be despatched for a lamb which could be sacrificed for the good of the patient.

The wife of the man demurred and suggested that the company should at least await the morn before embarking on such desperate measures.

It was easy to understand her concern. Chickens,

charms and potions cost money or its equivalent and already she had mortgaged a goodly part of her household goods in acquiring remedies for her man.

Whether or not it became necessary to slaughter a lamb I shall never know, because I thought it expedient to change my quarters. I could do little more. I could not possibly have intruded into the circle around the sick man, even though I was aware that the treatment he was receiving was probably hastening him to his death.

Indeed, his friends and neighbours evidently worked with thoroughness, for I was told, early the next morning, that the man was dead.

Going to collect the belongings which I had left in the house the previous night I found that this was indeed so. The poor widow was bewailing her lot. I could only attempt to console her by contributing to the burial fund.

A long strip of muslin had been resurrected from somewhere; and from the smell of camphor which it gave off it was reasonable to assume that it had been used at more than one burial already. The body of the man was wrapped in this shroud and it would be little more than this which he would require.

Later that day I saw the remains being carried away in a rough wooden box – for the dead have to be interred quickly in the East.

The box was carried from the house by the friends who had done so much to expedite the man's end; they performed this service not from any sense of remorse, but because those who act as pall-bearers acquire great merit.

As the cortège proceeds, the first person of the same religion who is met is expected to relieve one of the mourners and thus the burden is shifted from shoulder to shoulder until the burial place is reached.

The coffin or box, with the shawl which is placed over

it, are not interred. These are hired for the occasion by the poorer people and returned to the hirer after the body has been placed in a deep grave with only the muslin shroud as a cover. A priest was hurriedly summoned to recite from the New Testament in Arabic.

At yet another village I came across an occurrence which was more pleasing – nothing less than a wedding. The ceremonies attaching to marriages differ from country to country, sometimes in vital respects; sometimes in lesser. Invariably, however, they are of interest to onlookers, if not always for the principal participants.

Here the wedding is divided into two distinct ceremonies – the actual betrothal and the wedding ceremony proper. In Moslem law, both ceremonies are legal and binding. Consequently, there is more involved in the initial function than the lighthearted bestowal of a ring which may, or may not, already have adorned the finger of some earlier fiancée.

The ceremony of betrothal is a very serious one, into the preliminaries of which the families of both contracting parties have entered with zest, for it is one requiring the exercise of much business acumen.

Quite often betrothals are arranged by marriage brokers, many of whom are old women. They receive a commission from the two parties for their services. Much the same practice is observed by many of the Jewish fraternity, even in London, and it has not been unknown, I was told there on good authority, for Mayfair hostesses to receive a valuable 'present' for arranging a match between some wealthy social aspirant and a member of the peerage. The arrangement in every instance is mainly commercial.

The peoples of this part of the East, however, have one practice which may or may not commend itself to brides of other nations.

In the betrothal ceremony which I witnessed, the bride-groom-to-be was the Sheikh of the village and the girl the daughter of a neighbouring chief. They were not wanting in worldly goods, especially as the bridegroom's father was also a merchant who had journeyed to England and had taken to himself a Feranghi, a Frankish wife. But of that more presently.

The bride, her mother and other feminine friends were accommodated in one room while the bridegroom and his friends occupied one adjoining.

The presiding elder (he is not a priest: marriages are civil contracts) took up a position in the doorway between the two rooms and read from a list detailing the property of the bride.

It had not been prepared merely to impress the neighbours and the friends of the family, or from any sense of false pride. There was a real purpose to this part of the proceedings.

All the articles named by the elder were to give her a sense of security. In later years, should the man desire to divorce the bride, he would be unable to send her away penniless. He would have to provide her with all the goods and chattels mentioned in the list.

This practice may seem curious to some Western minds; nevertheless, it has its counterpart in Western marriage settlements. In Germany especially, it is frequently the practice for the groom to cite in his marriage settlement the cars, the houses and other items which one day *might* come into his possession. There is a close association between the two forms of contract.

I remained in this village long enough to witness the second part of the ceremony, since this took place only a few days after the first.

The bride lived in a flat-roofed single storey house and,

in common with half-a-dozen other such structures, it looked out upon a courtyard. In Europe you would say that it was but one of a collection of cottages which shared a common backyard.

All the neighbours came to the assistance of the bride and freely loaned carpets which were laid over the stone slabs of the court. These loans were augmented with gifts of flowers with which the court was further decorated.

A huge tea-urn had been obtained and this was kept bubbling the whole day. It was greatly in demand; its only rivals being long pipes of sweet sherbet which were passed from hand to hand. The court, by the way, was given over entirely to the women.

The bride was attired in a new silk robe and her neck was adorned with a string of glass beads amongst which were interspersed a few gold and silver coins.

This trousseau was the gift of the groom – another pleasing practice, some fathers-in-law will say.

The bride had not disdained cosmetics. Her cheeks were rouged, her eyes had been blacked with kohl and her garments had been plentifully besprinkled with scent.

The hostess of the occasion – quite an old woman – seemed to be serving in a professional capacity. Obviously she augmented her income by providing her services in this way. No mere amateur could have carried off the role as did she.

As the guests entered the courtyard they peered around for this woman and then advanced upon her, enunciating the words: 'May this wedding be blessed.'

And the hostess, with supreme gravity, would respond: 'In the Name of God enter; your kindness in coming to assist us is indeed great.'

In the adjoining house, where the guests of the Sheikh were assembled, a somewhat similar scene was being enacted. Here, however, the masculine temperament made for a little more verve and vigour.

A wandering minstrel had been imported to amuse the guests and he sang songs in a shrill, minor key, the words of which were improvised to meet the needs of the occasion.

Masculine humour, at such events as weddings, is cruder and much more direct than the feminine, and judging from the roars of laughter which the minstrel produced from the guests and the obvious discomfiture of the groom on sundry occasions, the man was well worth his fee.

The entertainer's voice was shrill and piercing, and I could not but notice with amusement that, when he introduced some sally at the expense of the bridegroom, the feminine chatter from the nearby courtyard suddenly ceased, and the hidden audience there was patently listening to the words with appreciation.

Once even, the fair ones so far forgot themselves as to echo the boisterous laughter of the men when the minstrel had been particularly audacious.

The formal part of the ceremony – a brief affair – had taken place earlier in the day and the singing and the laughter and the drinking of tea, coffee and sherbet proceeded until a late hour. At dusk, candles and lamps were produced and the whole assembly was served with a repast consisting of coloured rice, mutton, pomegranates and sweets.

Later, as the party showed signs of breaking up, a medley of particularly efficient bandsmen appeared as if by magic, and the surrounding roofs of the nearby houses became crowded with those anxious to witness the final phase of the ceremony.

The male guests assembled around the groom as an

escort and a procession was formed which made its way
slowly to the home of the bride.

As the groom reached the threshhold of his bride's
abode a lamb was sacrificed, and then the bride was led to
the doorway and given over to the bridegroom amidst the
plaudits of the spectators and the raucous blowing of
trumpets.

In all these proceedings, Sheikh Abdullah, the bridegroom's father was, I felt, taking but a half-hearted
interest. His mind, it would seem, was flying back to some
distant scenes, some former experiences. At first, I
thought that a man past middle age could hardly be
expected to raise enough enthusiasm about an affair which
warms young hearts; but the reason was different. He was
recollecting his own former, Ferangi, wife: the mother of
the boy whose wedding he was celebrating.

Until late that night I sat with him. Then he became
reminiscent. During the Great War, when European
countries were at each other's throat, he found a chance of
selling the wares of his land at a hundred per cent profit.
To make more money he went to England. He lived the
part, and began his story in the present tense; and I will let
him relate it in his own way:

8

Anis Learns to Love

'To be sure the Inglis are mad, for there in London whose circuit is many miles, I have seen soldiers marching and countermarching. Yet they be so few. Many men wear hats of felt even as in Kurdistan, called "bowlers", but they are pale of face and make much of the forbidden wine and pork. Yet the women are of an admirable fairness. These women are more warlike than the men, even as in Arabia, and their eyes are the colour of turquoise set in cheeks of coral. With a harem of such, the men of the desert might conquer the world.

'In the space of a few days I was made at home both by the Inglis and by men of my own country, now in London. All spoke of wounds and war, yet I was taken to a place on a hill called Hampstead, where many men and women met together to dance. Had he seen them, my father would have used his sword, for the men were pale of face and "precious".

'I knew nothing of "precious" until my guide – a woman with false teeth and smelling of strange flowers – explained that this meant "too proud to fight". By Allah! Within five minutes I might have strangled them all! Some men there were (whom at first I thought women) who had cheeks like cherry blossoms. They swayed from the hips as I have seen the dancers of the Nile, and I greatly regretted the absence of my Arab knife.

'All were drinking wine – deep, blood red. Glasses were on every table and I was sickened by the heat and smell of strange scent. Then at one side I saw an Inglis lily. Tall she was, unaccompanied by any man. Her eyes met mine and she smiled. Her shameless skirt showed legs clad in silver silk and I dared not look at her breasts cradled in a wisp of tinselled fabric. O Allah! That there should be such beauty and yet no man to possess it and keep it from sight of the common herd. Her eyes tugged my heart-strings. Without a word I pushed between the dancers and so came upon her, seating myself on the divan at her side.

'"I do not know you," she said. "But you look as though you might be worth it. Are you an Indian?"

'So I explained that I was of those who swept with the mighty Arab lancers in the conquests, up to India, possessing all the land, the riches, the women – all that pleased our kingly eye. She smiled, and her teeth were whiter than the snows of the mountain ranges. She asked whether I danced, whereat I said I would rather fight or make love. Her eyes met mine, blue as the sea I had left, and as seductive.

'"Let's sit outside," she said. "I cannot stick this crush. Mabel always has the most impossible people. Most of them are 'conchies' or 'indispensable' men in Government offices, drawing umpteen quid a week."

'The gardens of the Inglis are very beautiful, and here was one where seats were cunningly hidden between arbours of roses. We sat upon a seat and presently my Lily laid her hand in mine.

'"You're rather a dear," she said.

'This I took for a sign of favour, and felt the blood leap in my veins. From her came the scent of violets at dawn as

I have smelled them a thousand times under the morning star. Yet I felt at a loss.

'An Inglis would have known what to do. I knew what my pulses told me; to sweep her into my arms, to crush her slender form so that it melted into mine, to carry her away and possess her utterly and most beautifully.

'Nevertheless, I was in a strange country and afraid. Moreover, who can tell the heart of a woman?

'"You don't even know my name," said my Lily. "You'd better get it straight, in case any questions are asked. What with sitting out here and with an unknown Sheikh, I'm likely to lose what reputation I've got. Not, of course, that that would trouble me. Reputations are like the bloom of life, so darned fragile that they are not worth keeping!"

'Still I did not know what to do, save that the girl slipped closer to me so that I could see the sweet hollow between her breasts. I tore my eyes away, for here lay madness. The blood was singing in my ears and there was a red mist in front of me which hitherto had come only when I saw my knife sink home in an enemy's throat.

'"I'm Nella Carson," I heard her say. "Rising twenty-three, sound in wind and limb and – er – a widow." She leaned forward so that I could not see her face.

'"Jim was killed out in Salonica fifteen months ago. Things happen like that, you know. For a time I thought the end of the world had come, but now – oh well, I've grown wiser. Bloody world, isn't it?"

'In that moment I craved to comfort her. Tears were slipping down her cheeks and I, who knew the lore of the rifle and the knife, felt powerless. Yet at last I turned to her, and, as it were a miracle, found her in my arms. I had known her perhaps half an hour. Yesterday I had never seen her, yet at that moment my heart was in my throat with the fragrance of her.

'"Tell me," I whispered, "may I not comfort you?"

'Then I found her lips, petals of purest passion that clung to mine and swept me to Paradise. Allah be praised that women are women, whether in Baghdad or Hampstead. She lay cradled in my arms, her slender limbs against mine, and I could feel the throb of her heart as I bent to kiss the scented whiteness of her shoulder. How long we sat in that garden of the *houris* I do not know.

'It must have been long, for when we returned many of the "precious" men had left, taking their women with them. Almost alone in the ballroom my Lily found our hostess, who smiled sweetly.

'"Quite a conquest!" I heard her say. "You really must be a trifle more discreet though, Nella dear. You never know what these foreigners will do!"

'Whereat I would have killed the woman, had I not received a soft glance from blue-eyes that wrenched my heart even as a cook wrenches the neck of a chicken.

'"Will you see me back?" said my Lily, when we were under the stars again.

'A street stretched empty before us. Few lights showed, but of a sudden a taxi-cab slowed beside us. So it was we went home together. I did not know the hour, for time has naught to do with passion. In a rose and amber drawing-room she showed me photographs – her man, her father, her sisters. So I came to know somewhat of her life, for now it appeared she worked in London alone. A question burned in me, so that I could no longer stifle it.

'"Have you children?" I said. "Perhaps a son to follow in the steps of your husband? Surely he would be a great fighter."

'My Lily lay back, the lamplight making her an elf, rose and silver clad. I saw her smile.

'"Do remember you are in London," she said, "and also that I was the wife of an infantry subaltern. Children are a luxury we could never afford."

'I did not understand her, save that perhaps she was unfortunately afflicted of Allah. Presently I rose to take my leave, whereupon she leapt to her feet.

'"Come and see me again," she whispered.

'It is not well to kiss the women of the Inglis. No man – save he be a fool or a hero – brings himself within their wiles. Maybe I am a little of both, for when I walked down that dark road in the starshine with my heart singing, I knew I was in love. What then would my father, the old Sheikh, say?

'A Ferangi woman, even though fair as the dawn? And the greybeards? And the women of my father's harem? What place had she in the life of a warrior of the desert, where death lurks at every corner and women are the lawful spoil of the strongest?

'After a while and with many questionings I came to my house. Allah preserve me from living in such a wilderness of houses so that scarce a tree can be seen and there is only the stench of petrol! So I lay upon my bed that night, and for many nights afterwards.

'First I put the thought of that seductive one away from me. Then I gloried in her beauty. I could neither eat nor sleep. My strength departed from me. Then the spirit that lives in the wires rang a bell, and a servant came to tell me that a woman wished to speak with me. For me there was but one woman, and at her voice my heart leaped into my throat so that I could remember not one word of the Ferangi tongue, in which I was by now becoming more adept.

109

'"That you, Anis?" her voice came from the machine. "What's been biting you? Got anything on tonight? Good. Then come and call for me at seven o'clock. I've got seats for a show and afterwards – perhaps . . ."

'The silver voice ceased, while I could say nothing.

'"Did you hear? Can you manage it?"

'Then I spoke burning words into the telephone, so that I heard a soft, faint laugh and then a click.

'That night was the first of many. With my Nella, I grew to know, to understand and afterwards to love a little this great London. From restaurant to restaurant we went. Or I would hire a car and we would slip down a wide road called the West towards the Thames, where were boats which I knew not how to manage. At first, I tried to hire a servant who should row, but Nella thought not. Indeed, she herself did propel a punt in most skilful fashion, whereat I grew shamed, since of this thing I knew nothing. But of those nights when lights danced upon the black water I scarce dare speak. The whisper of leaves shrouding us from the common gaze, the dark ripples that swept past our fingers like those waves of passion which engulfed us. My Nella cared for nothing save that I loved her, and in her arms I found heaven.

'"Darling – what are we going to do about it?"

'In those few words I faced the crisis of my life. Of Ferangi fashions I knew nothing, save that by the paying of money and the mumbling of a priest a wife can be made. And such a wife! A thing of flame and silver, fragrant as the dawn, whose lips snatched me up to Heaven so that the blood thundered at my ears and I knew that only in her wonder could I find satiety and peace.

'"*What are we going to do about it?*"

'The Ferangi know naught of the language of love. Maybe that is why their women speak of a sixth sense, for I have known many red-faced officers of theirs and others to whom words come with difficulty, save only when they are angered. Yet now with her lips under mine I knew the answer.

'"Tell me, light of my eyes!" I whispered. "Rose of my heart, do with me what you will so that you come to me soon. Let nothing stand between us, neither money nor custom. How shall we do this thing?"

'My Lily sighed, resting her bright head against my shoulder.

'"It's not so easy, old thing," she said. "I have got a father, also aunts. And what they will say when they hear I am marrying a scion of the great Sheikhs I daren't think. Why *will* people always judge things from the viewpoint of fifty years back, instead of in the light of the present? *'We never did things like that in our day!'* I can hear Aunt Agatha saying. As if she ever did anything more than squeeze a curate's hand and imagine that put her on the slippery hill to Hell!"

'Of such talk I could make little, but it served to fire my blood. If her father was indeed unwilling that his daughter should mate with a man of high Arab blood, my way was plain. I should seek him out, yet deal tenderly with him. There would be no need of a knife. No need, even, of a stranglehold. I should talk with him as men of the desert have talked for a thousand years, and doubtless he would see sense.

'"How much money have you got?" said my Lily after a pause. "Please don't misunderstand me. I don't care a damn whether you are a millionaire or a beggar. And I only want to know your immediate resources. Could you manage a special licence, or shall we say banns? That'll take three weeks, you know. And you are apt to be a bit impatient, aren't you?"

'So I was initiated into the mysteries of marriage as practised by the Ferangi. For my Lily I forswore my traditions, my very life. Think ill of me if you will, that as a strict Moslem of the Arabian lands I should mate with the Infidel. I make no plea, save that I was in love and so driven, could do naught save bow before a greater force.

'For three Sundays I attended a great place of worship where many men and sweet-smelling women came to pray. Such music I have never heard, and pray I may not have to endure again, for it seemed ill to ears accustomed to the music of mountain and stream, of wind whispering in upland forest. It was close to the shrieking of she-camels. Yet I said naught, seeking to pleasure my loved one.

'Hand in hand we sat and listened to an Inglis of mournful aspect. Of what he said I heard little, except that he spoke of the wrath to come. He seemed to relish its prospect. Yet he clearly knew little of wrath, an undersized man whom I could have crushed with a single blow.

'The God of the Ferangi may be powerful, but his priests are pale and thin-bellied. Truly a poor lot! Yet it was with this very man that my Lily and I gained a passport to Paradise. Witnesses there were, from the house in which I lived.

'The sun shone, but no more brightly than the eyes of my beloved, and within twenty minutes she was mine. In a dark room on one side of the church I gave money to the priest and his underlings. Then my name and that of my Lily was inscribed in a great book, whereupon all wished us joy, and even the driver of the taxi-cab loosened his brutish features. The whole world smiled upon us, and so we came to a hotel where my Lily had taken rooms.

'There are some who say that London is a place of grime and penniless people. Yet here we found only much kindness, great happiness, and an eagerness to help us on our way.

'Truly, certain – if not all – of the Ferangi are kind of heart, belying their frozen outward looks. Thus it was that, within six weeks, I entered into Paradise.

'When I had come to London I had had no thought of this, yet now for the first time in my life I had a woman who lay against my heart, a thing of warmth and tenderness which demanded and gave love in overflowing measure.

'Yet often in the night I thought of the men of the desert, of my father and the Elders. What they would say of this I dared not think.'

In matrimonial bliss Anis forgot the War; he stayed on and on in England; he extended the export business to Damascus. A year passed and more; and then the nursing home gave him the sad news of his wife's sudden death in childbirth. Ali he named the motherless boy; and Ali, the son of the English bride, grew to manhood in the purest desert traditions, in his father's land, to wed the only daughter of his father's rival Arab chieftain. And Ali talked only in terms of Arabia, in the spirit of that which is best in Islam, carrying the mantle of his father not unworthily.

When the young man came in to say good-night and kissed his father's hand in token of thanks for getting him a wife, a happy light ran in the eyes of the old Sheikh. In jest, I asked Ali whether he would like to visit England.

'No!' said the bridegroom emphatically. 'No, I shall not go where they eat pig and drink wine!'

While on the subject of marriages, I might just as well refer to another wedding which I presently saw among the Kurds. Here also, the marriage arrangements are made between the parents, the father of the groom invariably making a substantial present to the father of the bride.

This present usually takes the form of cattle or household produce, as the Kurds of the countryside have little use for money as such. Much, of course, depends upon the comeliness and the status of the bride, but before parting with his daughter in marriage a father can expect to receive four or five sheep and perhaps one or two goats thrown in, to lend weight to the bargain.

Even after the wedding contract has been cemented by these gifts, the bride's father has, by custom, to stage a display whereby he can demonstrate his unwillingness lightly to part with the precious, honoured daughter of his house.

In this and in the actions of the groom, something of old-world romance and chivalry is pleasantly present.

When the time of the wedding ceremony comes around, the groom's father gathers as formidable an array as is possible. He collects his warriors and his friends, and the groom is attired in a striking garment of many colours.

A procession is formed and with much brandishing of swords and firearms, an advance is made on the bride's home. As they approach, garish musical instruments are played and much ammunition is fired from the ancient guns.

This is a signal to the bride's father, who must now sally forth with his own band of warriors and friends and engage the advancing 'foe' in mock combat.

To an ordinary and uninitiated onlooker, the battle appears to be a sanguinary one, and it is in one's mind to be somewhat sorry for the groom. After all, one reflects, the bargain has been made and the presents handed over, yet his father's forces are repulsed again and again.

This, however, is all part of the ceremony.

Eventually the defenders give way and the groom is allowed to rush to the bride's home and bear her off in triumph, amidst the banging of cymbals, the roar of musketry and the triumphant cries of his 'army'.

The bride's father still has a part to fill.

He must detach himself from his vanquished warriors and rush headlong after his daughter and beseech her to return. If she were to acquiesce, I imagine that a real battle would ensue, but she invariably refuses.

Then the two forces combine, and all repair to the bride's home for the wedding feast, and the night is spent in singing and dancing.

On the stroke of midnight, the groom appears with horses, to carry the bride away to her new home.

9

To the City of Caliphs

You must assume that while you have been reading these sociological sidelights, I have been steadily plodding my way towards the Iraqi frontier.

The country through which I passed at this stage of my journey was the reverse of interesting: much of the desert ground being covered with lava and the whole prospect monotonous and uninviting.

Water often became a matter of serious moment, but fortunately I am a seasoned vagabond and I know how to take care of myself and my pack animals.

Before departing on my adventure, I had had fashioned a stiff canvas bag with a mouthpiece and a variety of straps attached.

This I rescued from my assortment of luggage, filled with water and suspended it from the martingale support of one of the mules and from the saddle girth. The water-filled canvas bag thus passed between the animal's forelegs and, as a burden, caused him no inconvenience.

I regret to say, however, that the water itself seriously disturbed both the mule and me on some of those long marches between wells; for, as the animal ambled along, the contents of the bag swished from side to side with a most seductive and almost a lascivious sound: which made me think of the story of Tantalus and much else.

What made matters worse was the fact that the canvas bag was slightly porous, and the movement and the percolation made the water most delightfully cool: though at the cost of a constant loss of water.

I retain quite fond memories of that mule, even though he came to a sad end.

On one rather dreadful march, when our water supply was all but exhausted, I had to take pity on the unfortunate beast and spare him a few drops of the fluid above and beyond the meagre ration he had had two hours previously.

I carefully decanted a little water into one hand and then, with the other, I caught hold of his lolling tongue. Carefully I poured the water onto this receptive organ and wetted it thoroughly with a gentle massage.

Thereafter that animal lost much of his 'mulish' complex. He seemed to sense that I had parted with something of really great value and he would amble after me tamely like a pet dog.

Poor fellow, sure-footed though he was, he slipped and fell one day among some boulders and broke a leg.

Mentally drawing two lines from ears to eyes, I had to shoot him where they crossed.

Within a short time, and before I had progressed a hundred yards from the scene, the carrion of the air were disputing with a couple of jackals for all that remained of him.

I make no special claim for the advantages of my canvas water bag, for the idea is quite well known among Easterners. Except in the large towns, and sometimes not always there, there are no drinking water plants. More often than not, water has to be taken from rivers and pools in a very muddy state and it has to be rendered drinkable.

This is done by a simple, yet ingenious process. A filter is used, constructed from clay in the shape of an Italian wine bottle.

The potter, when working the soft clay, introduces a little salt into it. The jar is then fired in the ordinary way, but when water is poured in, the salt dissolves, leaving minute holes through which the water percolates.

The most nauseating-looking water can be rendered clear by means of this filter which can be purchased for a tiny sum.

Whether or not we of the East have become immune to microbes, I do not know, but we seldom feel ill effects from drinking such water. Although rendered cool and clear by this simple process, microbes must still be there.

Europeans, who find themselves in like circumstances, are recommended to take the further precaution of boiling the water.

Boiled water is insipid and unsatisfying because the air has been largely driven out. Nevertheless, it is better than cholera or typhoid.

It is in this arid region that, now and again, one comes across some curious walled camps, ancient and fortified. They are constructed in the shape of pointed stars and have long-walled entrance roads.

It was here, during one of the periods when I was woefully short of water and by no means certain of my direction, that I saw a heavy aircraft on its way to Baghdad.

This machine of the moderns seemed incongruous in such surroundings, but I was glad to see it. Although it crossed my path at a tangent a considerable distance away, it gave me a much-needed sense of comfort and assured me that my general direction was right.

It must not, however, be imagined that all is dolorous and dispiriting on treks through country such as this. I can imagine nothing that would be better for the harassed dweller of the city racked by stress to the point of exhaustion and even mental instability. I have seen many such men in London ordered away from their business worries to the hectic gaieties of the south of France, when what they really needed was peace and solitude.

The life that I led at that period held a charm peculiarly its own. It was primitive, it is true, and it demanded perfect bodily health. As for 'nerves', their reaction is speedily blunted in such surroundings: by the wonderful tonic properties of the air and by healthy fatigue.

When one journeys by air or train, the short space of time spent passing between places of 'interest' is but a boring interlude. It is a time of irksome inanition during which one's routine is suspended.

But on such treks, out in the vast distances, one's real existence was upon the move and the brief stay in each stopping place, a period of preparation for the next lap in the journey and also a much needed rest.

The routine of such a life is a little irksome at first for most city-bred Europeans, but it is easily learned.

Each twenty-four hours in the rural parts of the Arab lands is divided into four natural, but unequal, parts.

There is the period of hurry and activity in the early morning, followed by a longer one of comparative tranquillity on the march. Then follows the bustle attendant upon arrival and then the period of beautiful dreamless sleep.

And what sleep! Especially if it be under the stars, out in the desert.

119

Here the desert can be both friend and foe. The traveller has to remember that it quickly loses the heat that it absorbs during the day and that even during the summer nights it can become uncomfortably cold.

But, some will say, how nice to nestle into the soft, comforting sand! All have heard of the shifting sands of the desert, but one really needs to lie on them to realise how they can shift around a recumbent and sleeping human.

They can form little hillocks as hard as rock and cause very serious discomfort to the human frame. One rises and feels oneself gingerly, meanwhile looking round for the assailant who has caused such an ache and assaulted one with a big stick.

But the shifting sands can easily be subdued. If one hollows out a hole into which one places one's hip, rolling and tossing in one's sleep is made impossible and the sands do not ruck up in retaliation.

The sands, it feels, like to sleep when nightfall cames and their shifting is only to escape the restlessness of the turbulent.

Sometimes when sleeping on the desert there are visitors. Maybe some mosquitoes arrive to inspect the intruder.

They dart, and hum, and hover and seek the more closely to give of their attentions.

The best thing to do in such circumstances is to pull a rug up over the face. If this renders the feet and ankles bare, the only thing to do is to pull it down again and stretch forth in the darkness for one's socks.

If these appendages have deteriorated on the journey and are less than they were when they left the hands of the maker, then the only course left, if one insists on being worried by such insects, is for the traveller to pack his

120

traps and proceed to the shops of Baghdad or Damascus or Cairo where they sell prettily labelled bottles filled with liquid which is guaranteed to stun the most robust of mosquitoes at the first sniff. Personally I have found that mosquitoes thrive most excellently on most such concoctions.

Quite often one has other visitors. More than once I have been awakened when sleeping in the desert, and have found at a distance of eight to ten feet, a semi-circle of brightly glowing orbs about one foot from the ground.

At first it seems uncanny, but one soon learns to realise that it is only a pack of jackals who have paid a friendly visit and a violent 'Sh-sh-sh' is sufficient to disperse these cowardly creatures.

Once I was foolish.

I threw a boot at the semi-circle of eyes.

The jackals vanished and, in the morning, so had my boot.

The jackals – they had eaten it!

Notwithstanding pleasant distractions such as these on my line of march, I admit that I was not altogether displeased when eventually, in the distance, I saw the waters of a great lake.

I was sufficiently sure of my direction to recognise it as Lake Habaniyya and not the Bitumen Lakes which lie some twenty miles to the west.

This lake is in itself remarkable in that, when full of water, it covers an area of one hundred and forty square miles. And Nature has constructed it to a special design. It is so made that it could form the basis of a huge irrigation scheme which would make Iraq one of the foremost granaries of the world. Immense sums of money would be required for such an irrigation project, but they would only be relative, for the area to be irrigated would also be immense.

The eyes of engineers must glisten as they scan the waters of this inland sea, pressing so invitingly for their attentions. When the River Euphrates is in flood, the level of the lake is lower than that of the river, and it is possible to pour into it the surplus waters, thus forming a vast, natural storage. Then, in the late summer, when the waters of the river decline and sink to a lower level than those stored in the lake, what would be more simple than to release the stored surplus and allow it to flow back into the river and from there to canals and the crops withering for the want of this priceless fluid?

When I first reached it, in the early nineteen-thirties, the flying machines on their way to and from Baghdad, purred gently and easily over this lake. I had to make the circuit of its shores. Eventually I stumbled upon the main motor-road from Damascus and presently came to Ramadi on the banks of the Euphrates. Here I was at the entrance to modern Babylonia.

My safe arrival by such a route as I had travelled occasioned some little surprise. It had been generally believed that robbers were active and that some had been on the look-out for me, not so much to rob me of my poor possessions, but to hold me to ransom for money which they supposed I had deposited in some Western bank.

If my bank manager should read these lines he will probably be as astonished as I was. The agents of the nomads had been led sadly astray regarding my ability to pay.

Later on, some unfortunate, bedraggled travellers did stumble in to Ramadi and the hair-raising story which they told was so blatantly far-fetched that even the most gullible film producer from Hollywood would have rejected it.

The poor people, nevertheless, had been thoroughly frightened, as well as robbed, so they could be excused if their imagination ran riot over the gruesome details.

Quite seriously they told of devilish tortures, forgetful of the fact that their bodies were still intact and unmarked.

Fright and a vivid imagination, however, will do much. I have actually seen a man, informed by the Hakim, the wandering doctor, that he is going to die, curl up on his mat and pass from this world. Organically, it was subsequently proved, there was nothing the matter with the man.

Apparently the hold-up had been staged with dignity. A crowd of rough-looking men had suddenly appeared and surrounded the party.

There was no wild galloping or firing of guns. Instead the bandit leader had quietly stepped forward and seized the bridle of the animal carrying the foremost traveller – an obese merchant named Suleiman. The last three days and most of the nights, Suleiman had spent on his little-used feet and he was now an object for commiseration.

'Verily,' wailed Suleiman to me, 'did I protest to this Shaitan that I and my companions were but poor wayfarers with nothing with which to propitiate such rich and mighty men of the desert.

'This robber, this devil, this despoiler of the innocent, would not believe me, though I swore by the beard of the Prophet.

'He said not a word, but looked at me with those soul-searing eyes of his, gave the bridle a shake and I, Suleiman a trader, respected and one of substance, was tumbled to the dust whilst the ruffians roared at my discomfiture.'

'And then . . .' I prompted.

'And then,' sobbed Suleiman, 'he raised a great foot and placed it firmly upon me.

'"Poor, are you, O fat one?" he said. "We will see what gives to you your comfortable girth." What rudeness! How dreadful a man!

'In the meantime, the train animals were being unloaded and my merchandise laid out for inspection. Fortunately I had disposed of much en route, but that which was there I naturally could still ill-afford to lose.

'Those who were with me were lined up with their backs to the proceedings and a huge man with a great sword stood behind them telling all that he would remove the nose of the first one who turned his head. They stood there, trembling like cowards,' added Suleiman, 'making no attempt to protect me, paying no heed to my cries of distress or to the overwhelming extent of my anguish.

'Implanting a foot more deeply into my entrails, the robber chieftain beckoned over one of his underlings. This man took his place and not only held me down as did his master, but leaned nonchalantly upon me as he serenely watched the process of plundering.

'Soon all the animals had been stripped and minutely inspected. Then back came the chieftain and he was in no good humour.

'"We have appraised your rubbish," he said belligerently, "and it comes to a total worthy perhaps of one little finger. Certainly it is not enough to save the protuberance which so coyly enfolds the foot of Husein here, nor is it enough to save your head, or your arms, or your feet, or your legs. You must pay!" he thundered.

'To the best of my poor ability I enlarged on my dire poverty and the penurious state of those who were with me, but this villain merely laughed in his beard.

'"Let the portly one arise," he said to the heavy-footed Husein, "and we will inquire further into his poverty."

'My cries of indignation went unheeded and despite my valiant struggles, I was shamefully assaulted and deprived of all my clothing. Naked I stood in the desert and it was then that that mean-spirited Kasim there had the temerity to turn his head and wallow in my degradation.'

'Wallow?'

'Wallow. He laughed!'

'But,' I observed, 'Kasim is still in possession of his nose.'

'Verily,' lugubriously agreed Suleiman, 'but the guard with the sword was also giggling: delighting in my discomfiture, and he failed to notice the waywardness of Kasim.'

'Perhaps,' I interjected, 'you were not sufficiently insistent in declaring your penurious state.'

'Insistent!' howled the indignant Suleiman. 'Repeatedly did I declare by all that I hold holy that I was as the beggar of the bazaar. Yet, this foul beast would take no heed.

'"For shame, fat-belly," he said. "Do you see in my eyes the innocence of the doe?"

'Verily, I did not. Rather did I espy the glowing rapacity of the vulture. Compounded by that of the rat, the jackal and the hog.

'"Come," said this robber, "I have heard such tales many times before. You must pay for your life and for the lives of those who are with you."

'Yet again I explained that my possessions had already been looted, that I felt as if my very skin had been stripped off already: but this man refused to listen to reason. Impatiently he turned.

'"Take one of those men," he commanded, "and we

will let the obese Suleiman know what we have in store for him."

'Two dreadful, uncouth creatures advanced at his bidding and, drawing their scimitars, they seized upon the yelping and cringing Kasim. Verily had vengeance come upon him for glorying in my degradation, but the cries which he made as he was assaulted with the flats of those great swords turned my bowels to water.

'I was not allowed to see the nature of his maltreatment, yet as Kasim's cries became fainter I could but surmise that his end was near.

'When all became silent and the robber's henchmen came with their blood-reddened swords, the bandit turned to me with an evil smile and said: "Come, fat one. Now it is your turn."

'Again was I roughly assaulted and my executioners stood before me, anxious to perform their master's bidding.

' "We will make you pay," emphasised this horrid man, "even if it is only with your life. But the payments shall be like those to the money-lender – protracted, irksome, and painful.

' "First," he said, "we will remove your nose, then we will slice away your lip and then . . ."

'But I had had enough. No mortal could have held out longer than I did, but, in the end, I had to pay. I promised the man a letter to a business friend on which payment would be made. I thought that if I could but escape from his clutches and send word to this friend to dishonour the note I could eventually seek the protection of the police.

'But that robber ruffian was too wily.

'After we had haggled and agreed upon a price he smilingly took the letter which I had penned and informed me that, were there any secret signs inscribed therein asking for assistance or suggesting any evasion, I would surely die.

'I had been sitting naked all this while, but as if in an act of great condescension he gave me back my garments. Then he sent a messenger away on a swift-trotting camel and informed me that I was still a prisoner. Most of the evening he devoted to telling me of the manner of the death which would be mine if his messenger, and the money, failed to materialise on the morrow.

'Fortunately for me, all went well. My business friend met my bill without suspicion and the messenger appeared in good time with my ransom.'

'And then,' I suggested, 'you were given your freedom and you made all haste to the nearest outpost and informed the authorities.'

Suleiman raised his hands despairingly.

'I was given my freedom,' he agreed, 'and that was all.

'"None of your tricks, fat one," said the bandit in parting. "I do not wish to be hunted over the desert by a Farangi aeroplane and sent to perdition by a rain of machine-gun bullets.

'"You are much too fat from rich living," he added, "and you need to lose weight, fat rather; therefore, I will repay the inconvenience that I have caused you. I will keep your animals, though they be but sorry specimens, and you can walk."'

'And did you walk?' I asked sympathetically.

'Indeed I did,' sighed Suleiman. 'For three days we staggered on our way here and I am near to death.'

Poor Suleiman!

He was indeed unfortunate, but I doubt whether he ever really missed the amount he was forced to pay as ransom. Despite his many protests, he was known to be a rich man.

And three days' hardship in the desert!

I had not the honour of Suleiman's acquaintance before his great tragedy, but I can attest to the fact that even after this dismal occurrence and the trials and tribulations which followed, he was still grotesquely obese. What could he have been like before?

Gradually, yet surely, desert raiders such as those who harried Suleiman are being stamped out and each succeeding day makes it more difficult for them to carry on their trade.

The Iraq police force does wonderfully efficient work in this and other respects, but there is no question of the fact that it is still incumbent upon travellers to take all precautions. The terrain favours the robbers.

The police have to patrol frontiers of some 2500 miles: and, in addition there are some 7,000 miles of motor roads, railways and navigable waterways. With such a vast area to cover, the difficulties of maintaining an adequate passport and police system can easily be imagined.

Mosul, with its population of some eighty thousand, comprising Christians, Arabs, Kurds and Turks, I have always found to be an insufferable place because of the heat – and I am well accustomed to extremes in temperature. I found, however, that in the hot season, even the regular inhabitants sought refuge in cellars during the day and spent their nights on the flat roofs. Those who went abroad during the hottest period of the day only did so in case of absolute necessity.

One puzzle still to be solved is how on earth this area could have become a centre of civilisation with such a climate. A glance at the map will show that Mosul is built on the west bank of the Tigris, more or less opposite the site of ancient Nineveh.

Some say that the climate has changed: but archaeological evidence belies this.

The radiation of heat from the walls of the houses has to be felt to be believed. It wells out in waves and this is not made the more pleasant when it is realised that not all the inhabitants have assimilated the most modern ideas regarding the disposal of garbage and sewerage.

Nevertheless the souks of Mosul are always interesting, although they cannot be compared with those of Istanbul, Damascus or Tabriz. A great deal of trade is done here, for it is the one real outlet for the commercial activities of a vast area.

One means of river communication is by rafts. These are constructed from inflated goat skins – hundreds of them – which are lashed together with willow branches.

These rafts, which are usually furnished with a cabin of sorts made of poles and gaudily coloured cloths, provide an easy and comfortable means of travel between Mosul and Takrit and beyond – that is, if one cares to forsake the motor-road which more or less follows the course of the Tigris for the whole distance.

At Mosul the Tigris is crossed by a bridge and immediately one comes to Koyunjik and the mounds that mark the site of the palace of Sennacherib in Nineveh.

From here, and gazing northward to the foothills some forty-five miles away, one can determine the position of Alqosh, even though it cannot be seen.

Alqosh was once the home of the prophet Nahum and little doubt is now entertained that this is the place where the prophecies of Nahum were written.

Unless the traveller is very keen I should advise him (or her) to take this much for granted, for although a motor-road connects Nineveh with Alqosh the latter place is little more than an insignificant village.

In the days of Nahum, however, it must have been a place of some social importance and, as a recreational centre, may have occupied a position very similar to some of the hill stations of India.

As the heat of the Indian plains drove those who could afford it (and quite a few who certainly could not) to Simla, Mussoorie, Dalhousie, and the like, so it has to be presumed that in the time of Nahum, the richer residents of Nineveh fled to the foothills to escape the summer heat. Nearby Alqosh would have provided a convenient place of temporary residence.

Probably also, Alqosh was the place where the old adage of 'idle hands' originated. I am not endeavouring to malign the hill stations of India, but were a modern Nahum to visit some of the wilder of them during the height of the season, I am afraid he would be just as unpleasant and as morbid as his ancient prototype.

The authorities must have sensed something of this during the two world wars, for there was at least one 'Indian hill station' to which British officers on leave from the vicinity of ancient Nineveh were forbidden to go!

In Alqosh, there is a small building where one is shown a scroll said to have been Nahum's. This is very difficult to believe, though there are signs that the building has been erected on a still more ancient site.

Near Alqosh, and in the general area of Mosul, there is a large community of Yazidis; numbering something over a quarter of a million.

These people are reputed to be devil-worshippers and they gave much trouble when the Turks held nominal sway in this area. That these people really worship devils I readily believed when I first came into contact with them.

No one else, I reasoned, would regard with such amazing equanimity, the enormous fleas which abound in their homes and which, with mosquitoes and flies, are frequently to be seen in dozens on the eyebrows and eyelids of children.

Boys and girls of nine or ten made no apparent effort to rid their faces of these disgusting insects. Quite unconcernedly they would allow the pests to browse away on their profiles while they asked the traveller a question or hung around in the hope of largesse.

It was near the home of that community that there occurred one of the greatest tragedies of my first visit there.

I had, for obvious reasons, found it vitally necessary to take frequent baths in a fast-moving mountain stream.

One day I was performing my ablutions when I trod upon a small rock which was being swirled along the river bed by the force of the current.

This disturbed a balance already made somewhat perilous by the presence of soap in my eyes, and I capsized.

Unfortunately, when floundering in the rapidly moving torrent I dropped my one tablet of soap – and it was germicidal soap at that.

I searched the river bed as well as I could, but did not recover it. Two especially unhappy days passed before I was able to make good my loss – two days and one ghastly long night – which I shall never forget; for sand or river silt makes a very poor substitute for soap.

Subsequent missions to contact the Yazidi priesthood, with the correct passwords, showed how very different things could seem from the inside of an organisation rather than looked at from outside.

The Yazidis, it was explained to me once I had established my bona-fides by means of a Sufi introduction, do

not worship the Devil at all. The accusation was started by
Turkish fundamentalists, who noted that they blacked out
the name of the Evil One from all writings. But the reason
they did this was not to give evil prominence, according to
their priests.

They have, of course, several beliefs and practices
which are in conflict with Islam, Judaism or Christianity,
the chief local religions.

Yazidis, for instance, have priestesses; they shun the
flesh of the pig but drink wine as a sacrament. Jesus was an
angel in human form, they say, who was crucified but did
not die on the cross. He will return: but his return is a
special, technical term for some special event.

Quite the most interesting of all, to me, was their explanation for the multiplicity of their beliefs and rituals. They
said that certain communities, all over the world, have
been entrusted with various rites, each one of which has a
certain value and which is to be 'activated' (made live is the
term actually used), as and when commanded by a supreme religious head. He it is who alone knows the real
meaning and use of rituals. For all other people, said their
High Priest (the Great Sheikh of Religion) to me, with an
amazing similarity to modern sociology, all rituals were
mere fossils, and had no spiritual, only a community and
emotional, use.

He said: 'God is not listening to such people; the people
are listening to each other. This has its uses. These uses
are not of God, but are of man.'

10

Black Magic in the Desert

Being interested in the occult, I took the opportunity of finding out the truth about the Black Art, said to be widely practised in this area of Iraq.

Magic and the study of the hidden sciences is known to be as ancient in the Arab lands as in any part of the East; indeed, it is not too much to say that the people of this area are the true successors of the magicians of old Egypt. Their name for Alchemy (Al Kemia) means simply 'The Egyptian Science', and, with the old Egyptians, they formerly believed that gold was a sovereign cure for all human diseases.

And 'magic' itself is supposed to come from the name of the Zoroastrian sages (also called kings), the Mages or Majuses of this area.

On this occasion when I travelled through Arabia, I took a great deal of trouble to discover whether any of the ancient arcane studies and occult ideas still remained among the people. I had previously read and discussed many volumes upon the occult lore of the Arabs of old, the works of Geber (Jabir), Al-Buni, and many others, and I was anxious to know whether their principles of alchemy, astrology and magic were still practised in the country.

I found that they were, but that their practitioners took

a great deal of unearthing. I am, of course, not alluding to mere fakirs or snake-charmers, but to veritable students of the arcane sciences. I was soon to discover that not much was to be gleaned in Arabia proper, or in the Hejaz, where the strictness of Moslem principle forbids any savour of the occult. It was, indeed, in various odd corners in which I found myself and in Syria north and south that I encountered that which I sought.

After much careful questioning, I was directed to the ancient city which was once the seat of a college of Chaldeans and Magi, and the alleged centre of the Orphic Mysteries. It was here I met my first alchemist, who received me in his house, clad in flowing robes.

After some skirmishing, he admitted that he was a practitioner of the art of Geber, and that he sought three things: the philosophers' stone, at whose touch all metal should become gold; the elixir of life, and the universal solvent which would dissolve all substances.

Indeed, he confided to me that he had discovered the last. I asked him in what he kept it, if it dissolved all things, and he replied 'in wax', this being the one exception.

The next day I was granted the unusual privilege of inspecting the alchemist's laboratory, and duly presented myself at the appointed time. My highest expectations were fulfilled; everything was exactly what an alchemist's workplace should be.

Yes, there was the sage surrounded by his retorts, alembics, crucibles, furnace, and bellows, and, best of all, supported by familiars of gnome-like appearance, squatting on the ground, one blowing the fire (a task to be performed daily for six hours continuously), one pounding substances in a mortar, and a third seemingly engaged in doing odd jobs.

Involuntarily, my eyes sought the pentacle inscribed with the mystic word 'Abracadabra', but here I was disappointed, for the arts of ceremonial magic had no place in this laboratory.

One of the familiars had been on a voyage of discovery to London where he had bought a few alchemical materials; another had explored Spain and Morocco, without finding any alchemists, and the third had indeed found alchemists in Algeria, though they had steadfastly guarded their secrets.

After satisfying my curiosity in a general way, I asked the sage to explain the principles of his researches and to tell me on what his theories were based.

I was delighted to find that his ideas were precisely those of the medieval alchemists, namely, that all metals are debased forms of the original gold, which is the only pure, non-composite metal. All nature strives to return to its original purity, and all metals would return to gold if they could. Nature is simple and not complex, and works upon one principle – that of sexual reproduction.

It was not easy, as will readily be believed, to follow the mystical explanations of the alchemist. Air was referred to by him as the 'vulture', fire as the 'scorpion', water as the 'serpent', and earth as something else; only after considerable questioning and confusion of mind was I able to disentangle his arguments.

Some little distance from there, among the foothills of Kurdistan, I unearthed another student of magic. He certainly looked the part and talked largely about magical operations, but, as I never saw him actually perform any, I cannot say whether he was merely a deluded disciple of the great art, or a very ordinary fraud.

This, however, I can say; that he assuredly knew more concerning magic and its procedures than any man I ever

Alone in Arabian Nights

met. He showed me how to form a magical circle, guarded
from the intrusion of jinn and evil spirits by the time-
honoured symbols, lights and perfumes; but when I asked
him to evoke the powers of the elements he bluntly refused, on the grounds that such an experiment required a
great deal of preparation lasting several days, and that it
was dangerous to attempt it without that.

I left his little house in the hills feeling rather disappointed, and observing a number of people, chiefly girls
and women, hanging about the doorway, I concluded that
he made his living by selling charms and philtres to them.

I afterwards learned that this was so, but I must admit
that he had a great reputation locally as a wizard and, while
conversing with him, I felt very strongly that he could
have carried out successfully at least some of the dark
experiments of which he spoke.

Later I discovered that this ability to create such an
impression was his chief strength.

I did not remain such a tyro for very long. I was under
instructions to collect and publish a survey of magical
practices, and I subsequently did so, in my *BLACK AND
WHITE MAGIC: Its Theory and Practice* (1952, 1953,
1975, etc.). The intention was to forestall a probable
popular revival or belief among a significant number of
people in this nonsense.

My son, Idries Shah, eventually completed this task,
when he researched for several years and published
two important books on the subject: a first-hand account
plus research work on the East, and a bibliographical
study of the main Western sources of magical literature:
ORIENTAL MAGIC (1956) and *THE SECRET LORE
OF MAGIC* (1957).

In Mosul itself there was a fair sprinkling of astrologers,

136

as befits the fame of the place and the proximity of the community of star-worshippers. There was also more than one occultist brotherhood.

But I experienced extraordinary difficulty in getting in touch with the members of one of the lesser-known fraternities. I succeeded in doing so at last, on the plea that I had journeyed many hundreds of leagues from India to join it, and indeed I would have become a member had I not failed badly in the tests of arcane knowledge which its members set me.

I thought that I had read and studied the mystical long enough to pass a fairly stiff preliminary examination in it, but I was not prepared for the standard set by the committee of this arcane society at Mosul. Of course, I say so humorously, for it was a debased standard.

Had their questions been based on the generally known facts of Sufism or even on Neoplatonic principles – as they claimed – I could have replied to them readily enough, but I could make little or nothing of the ideas connected with the corrupted system they believed was 'High Knowledge'.

These worthies, mostly elderly and very old men, had evidently, in the course of years, altered the process of arcane belief as understood in the Arab Middle Ages, into something so weird and wonderful that it was with difficulty I could refrain from laughing outright at some of the questions with which they plied me.

I found out afterwards, when we were drinking a friendly cup of coffee that their library consisted to a great extent of popular French works on the occult, such as one may pick up in Paris for a few francs.

So much for the magic of mysterious Mosul! Since then, of course, I have found the same thing very widely the case in Europe and the Americas.

But I should do the romantic old place a serious wrong if I did not admit that I actually discovered more than one real practitioner of the occult within its bounds.

I found at least three astrologers of repute in the city who might have stepped out of the seventh century. One of these shook his head sadly over the uses to which his science was put in England and elsewhere in the West. He was quite a good astronomer, too, and could descant learnedly upon starry lore much as Galileo might have done, and he had never heard of Einstein or Professor Jacks.

'Is there, or is there not, an astral influence on things or people?' he asked me bluntly. 'Who can deny it? Who dreams of doubting the influence of the sun on plants and on the health of man, or that of the moon on the tides? Even the humblest admit these things. The sun has an influence on the nervous system, sometimes for good, sometimes for ill. So much your science believes in. What is the Universe but a group of magnetic gloves which attract and repel each other? The creatures inhabiting them share in this magnetism and experience weal or woe from its operations. The several planets of the solar system exercise a magnetic influence upon each other, as scientists assure us. They must then also do so on the living beings inhabiting them. It cannot be otherwise.'

11

A Fight with a Horse-Thief

Coming southwards down Kirkuk way into Northern Iraq, I fell foul of Hatim, the greatest of all horse-thieves in Arabia. I had managed to spot the horse which, in the eyes of the judges at the fair, was beyond doubt the best animal in the whole show.

I knew that the man standing next to me at the time of bidding wanted that horse badly. There was one other who wished to possess it more than he: that was myself. And I got it in the end.

When the man said that he would get not only my horse but more from me, as he jumped into his saddle and rode away towards Kurdistan, I took it for little more than an empty threat.

How was I to know then that he was a brigand chief, through whose territory I must pass if I were to reach Baghdad? At the horse-fair, therefore, I made light of the incident.

When you are travelling at almost ground level, you meet plenty of people who will threaten almost anyone with everything.

Well, nearly ten days rolled by before the fun started in the wild reaches of the hills.

Then, one fine morning I missed the horse. The fast little jet-black Arab had been abstracted from his stable sometime between dusk and dawn, and no-one could account for the manner of his going. But I, having had some experience of bandits, and now being warned about my adversary, thought I recognised the method, and within an hour of the discovery of my loss, I was hot on the trail.

I could trace the beast's spoor for nearly a mile down a muddy valley, where it was lost in the grass. But from the last hoof-marks, I saw that it had been travelling almost due south. It behoved me to be careful, for I knew that it was this bandit's custom to bag any pursuers and their horses by waiting for them on the very trail they followed when chasing him.

So I tried a trick. A challenge. I slipped my rifle out of its holster and blazed twice into the air over the seemingly empty desert.

The effect was almost magical. The top of a bare head, thatched with wild black hair, popped up from behind a bush not thirty yards away. There was the crack of a rifle, and the new swagger astrakhan cap of which I was so proud flew from my head, drilled clean through.

It's odd how a thing like that can make a man more angry than the loss of a fortune!

'Blast you!' I yelled furiously. 'I'll have your life-blood for that. Haven't you any manners, dog?'

'My mistake, dear one,' yelled he in return. It was the thief, sure enough. 'I meant it for your head, but the wind's not quite favourable from this angle. Sorry.'

'You will be sorry, God willing, if I can get within five yards of you,' I howled. 'What about downing rifles and giving the weapons of the country a chance? Can you handle the Arab knife?'

'Try me. Are you on? Yes, well, here goes.' And throwing down our rifles, we started to crawl towards each other, armed only with the broad-bladed curved daggers which the Arabs know how to wield to such purpose.

'You're a rough one, but reckless! I'll give you that,' jibed the brigand, as we came within a few feet of each other.

'I am Hatim, known as The Terrible, and what might your name be? And where do you bury your dead?'

It is customary in Arabia, when fighting a duel or acting as a champion, to announce one's identity.

'And I am Ikbal, ibn Amjad-Ali, Shah, of the tribe of Hashim!' I responded. 'As for burying, don't worry about me. There's plenty of space in the desert when the jackals and carrion birds have finished with you. They don't care what your name is.'

It's not a nice job to have to try to stick one of the sons of the desert in the gizzard, but when that one is a thief and behaves to you like a demon, and comes all the way from Kirkuk to the lower sands to steal a horse and more – well, there's little else left to do.

He jumped high as I rushed in, and played a trick I hadn't seen yet – a slashing downward blow to the base of the neck, just the thing to cut the spinal cord clean in two – a sort of brigand's dagger rabbit-stab, if you know what I mean.

But it didn't quite come off, and with a lurch upward from the knee, I suggested an operation for appendicitis.

The blood was pouring down my neck, and it wasn't like refreshing rain. The worst of the jambiyya is that when it strikes at all, it's bound to leave a bad notch at the best. It was really only a nasty slice, but it felt as though he had got home between my vertebrae.

Then the brigand pretended to stumble. I was just about to strike downward behind his left shoulder – a difficult break for the blade, which is built for frontal fighting – when his head collided forcibly with my chin. Now this isn't in the rules, and I yelped my protest as I fell.

'No Mosul City effete stuff here,' growled he, as he bore me down and raised his knife with a flourish. 'This is where you get it in the neck, you twisting double beast.'

'Liar!' I choked. 'You know that's not true. You strike a bad patch at the horse-fair and feel you've got to blame somebody, and look about for a victim.'

I don't mind being blamed for anything I've really done, but . . . since there weren't any rules now, I struck upward with my knee and caught him well amidships before he could bring the blade down. Then I buried the knife deep in his breast – or thought I did.

I rose and made to survey the corpse. How was I to know that the brigand wore a coat of mail? Beneath his rather disreputable clothing – he had on one of those bullet-proof waistcoats which Birmingham turned out. Made of the finest steel, which looks almost like silk, the garment has almost the protective capacity for a human that armour-plating has for a battleship.

And as I rose, the 'corpse' rose also, and emitting a wild war-whoop, slashed savagely at my throat. So surprised was I at his sudden rejuvenation that only the biggest, instinctive backward jump I ever managed saved me from annihilation.

Then we closed, and I guessed how it was.

'You dog!' I cried. 'You challenge me to a knife-fight and wear a steel singlet. D'you call that fair fighting?'

'Sorry,' he said. 'I'll equalise things. I only donned this as an insurance against backbiting, sniping you know, from the bedouin. They don't always want to face you.'

Throwing off his rather dirty upper garment, he tore the steel mesh off his shoulders and faced me once again.

Then I did something which appealed to him. I flung down my knife, and, remembering the boxing I had been taught at a British university, I made a shape and struck out at his jaw.

He obviously knew something of the noble art. Down on the turf went his blade, and he squared up to me. We sparred for a bit, but there was no referee to separate us and we closed.

Here he was scarcely a match for me, for there are no wrestlers like those of the Afghan mountains. For perhaps thousands of years we had used wrestling as an exercise, in peace and war. I was known as one who had reached the quite respectable grade of 'Eagle'.

Crash onto the springy yellow turf he went, and – with the noise of a hammer striking a nail – his head cracked on one of the treacherous patches of whinstone which crop up all over this desert country. He lay there, seemingly dead as a stone, blood streaming from his forehead.

I bound up the Terrible One's head as well as I could, and looked about for his horse. But I could espy neither his well-known chestnut nor my stolen black Arab. So I caught my own mount and managed to lift him into the saddle with some difficulty. Then I jumped up behind and steered southwards.

But I had forgotten the wound in my neck. Getting into the saddle had opened it again, and I could feel the blood pouring down my back. The galloping of my animal made matters worse. I began to feel faint, and grabbed at the beast's mane. In doing so, I disturbed the man's balance, and down we both came to the ground.

When I came to once more it was night and I felt too weak and stiff even to move. On my shoulder lay a head. The head groaned.

'Can't you kill a man outright: without so much clumsiness? Where do you come from, anyway?' the brigand asked.

'Same to you,' I moaned. 'You can't use an Arab blade for peanuts. That slash you gave me across the back of the neck was as amateurish a stroke as ever was. The answer to your question is that I happen to know because my ancestors were experts with the jambiyya when yours were still in Kurdistan.'

'Well, we're both in the same trouble now,' he whispered weakly, 'and there's no hospital near, you can bet on that. So there we are. It's rather a disgrace that I should die without falling in actual combat, isn't it? I cannot call to mind any of my ancestors who did that.'

'I'm afraid we're booked for heaven, unless they come to look for us,' I replied, 'and there's not much chance of that, because I am on my own. But let's end friends, Hatim, The Terrible. Let's call it quits, and forget the horse. We can let the animals loose, and they may find people and water by themselves.'

When I explained that the horse which I had bought was to be given to a shrine, for which both he and I had great reverence, the brigand was more mortified than ever.

'May the holy shrine forgive me,' he groaned. 'Well, wayfarer, I apologise. All this blood-letting and playing the bandit for nothing!'

Just then we heard voices, and raised a feeble shout. The newcomers were a small band of pilgrims, forced-marching through the night to make up for some lost time.

They got us to a doctor; and in a week I was my own man
again. It took Hatim nearly a month to recover, and in that
time we became bigger friends than ever. And both of us
alleged   that   we   had   been   set   upon   by
brigands.

I have heard from Hatim; he is now a peaceful citizen,
happily settled as an agricultural colonist near the foothills
of Kirkuk.

12

Awakening of Arabia

When I reached Baghdad again, I found the air thick with international politics; for it was more than a rumour that a Grand Arab Conference was to be held there soon.

The lumbering cultural mass of Islam, which had extended from southern France to China, from Central Europe to southern Africa, had been in retreat since the fifteenth century, closely followed by the expansionism of the European colonial powers.

Then came the First World War, and the abolition of the Caliphate. This legal fiction had held that the Turkish emperors stood at the head of the vast community of Islam: dispensing justice and protecting the lands and ideals of the believers. In fact, the very existence of the moribund Ottoman Empire had meant that nobody apart from the Colonial Powers did very much. What they did, of course, was to colonise.

In the enormous territory of Islam, only two or three nations were effectively independent: Afghanistan, Iran, and a truncated Turkey.

The victorious Allied Powers in 1918, most of them colonial ones, were of a mind to continue in their own sweet way. But the colossal effort to defeat Germany and the Central Powers, in 1914-18 as in 1939-45, almost fatally debilitated the European empires.

The Arabs started to develop their own nation-states, mainly on the pattern of Western ones. At the same time, the very powerful sense that all Arabs were one, should be united and free, pervaded the whole Arab World.

Less than a year after the Arab Conference held in 1931 at Jerusalem, the King of Iraq had resolved to convene another, on a similar model, in his own capital. Where the Grand Mufti had failed, he might succeed, for, in the opinion of many observers, the earlier Palestinian Conference was too localised in character. It over-emphasised, it is said, the Jewish-Moslem question, harped a little too much on the problems of pious foundations, the establishing of schools, inter-relationship of culture, and on such rather slight endeavours as the compilation of Anglo-Arabic dictionaries. Hence the first Conference in Jerusalem lacked a wider Moslem or Arab appeal. And the delegates fell out, to boot.

Subsequent Arab interaction was of a more constructive sort. It sought to explore the broader principles of co-operation amongst the Arabic-speaking peoples. It tried to consolidate an essentially Arab position, and sought to establish good neighbourliness with the Western Powers. The latter still effectively ruled most of the Arab World: the British in the Gulf, Yemen, Egypt and elsewhere; the French in much of North Africa and Syria; the Italians in Libya.

I attended many conferences of the Arabs and the Islamic world, generally as an observer; and later myself sent representatives to even more. We found that the intense individualism of the Arabs, as well as outside factors, made progress slow.

In the evolution of their past history, the Arabs have

certainly been divided, but it is a moot point whether any severe rift has split them to the point of hopeless irreconcilability. The Arab revolt against the Turks in World War I would have come even without British help, for every son of the desert considers himself charged with a national mission. With these patent facts before us, we should dismiss the idea that what occurred in Arabia during and after the First World War was any real index to the mind of those people. The War merely created an opportunity. It was a period of great excitement, of giving vent to old grudges in which foreigners did not hesitate to join.

The thought of a great federation of Arabia was never out of the Arab mind.

Perhaps the earliest indication of the Arab national movement is to be found at Beirut in 1860, when a newspaper called *The Syrian Trumpet* began to publish articles exhorting all Arabs to unite for a national federation. When *The Shield* blared in large type its motto, 'Love of Our Country is an Article of Faith', it caused the Turkish administration much concern.

It was Syria, too, that ultimately helped the younger Turkish party, in order to promote the Arab point of view of a national unity. But the first definite proclamation of the Arab committee was made in 1905, in which its members evinced a desire to unite all Arabia and to break away from Turkey.

They proposed a liberal constitutional monarchy under an Arab king, making the holy places of Islam in Mecca and Medina an independent State, and its king the Caliph of the Faithful. Again in the autumn of 1914, the leaders of Arab nationalism arranged a Congress of princes and tribes in Kuwait. Talib Bay of Basra worked for the idea, and was markedly successful in approaching the Emirs

and Chiefs of Nejd, Jabal Shammar, Kuwait, Muhamma-
rah and the representatives of the great Muntaifik tribes of
southern Iraq.

In the meantime, the European powers were not idle.

The Germans had been pouring men and material into
the desert. Their active propaganda was being furthered
in Yemen and Iraq, and in order to checkmate it, a secret
Anglo-French agreement was signed on 16th May, 1916.

In this, the French recognised that in the Arabian Peninsula England possessed 'a special political interest'; and
thenceforth Great Britain went deeper and deeper into the
Arabian mire by financing both King Husein of the Hejaz
in the south, and Sultan Ibn Al Saud, of Nejd in the north:
sworn enemies of one another. Some £6,000,000 (then a
colossal amount) was paid to the former and the latter was
subsidised to the extent of £5,000 a month, right into the
mid-1920s.

Curious situations arose from time to time. The battle of
Turabah between Husein and Ibn Saud was fought in May
1919, when both parties were receiving secret subsidies
from Britain; one from the Foreign Office and the other
from the India Office.

The only apology for these blunders which has been
given is that the Allies wished to remove all Turkish
control from Arabia. That, of course, had been done by
the Turks themselves as soon as they came under the wise
leadership of Mustafa Kemal.

The very first article of the Turkish National Pact of
28th January, 1920, was to acknowledge the independence of Arabia; and ever since there has been no difference of opinion between the two. The British subsidies to
the Arab leaders went on for years afterwards.

The struggle between the rivals for Arabian peninsular
power – Saud and his Wahabi puritans versus Husein of

the Hashemites – certainly continued, and there was fierce fighting all over the Arabian peninsula. But, in the main, whether Hashemites or people of Nejd, both always had the idea of Pan-Arabism at the back of all their struggles.

When Sharif Feisal was received by the Council of Ten at Versailles in February, 1919, as the representative of the Hejaz, he put forward claims for an Arab federation. Ibn Saud, the Sultan of Nejd, almost to the day, was haranguing his Wahabi followers on the same subject of Arab nationhood and unity.

But King Husein went a step further by proclaiming himself the Caliph, when the Angora Assembly banished Prince Abdul Majid in 1924. It seemed, too, that the consolidation of an Arab federation under the Hashemite banner was complete when both Palestine and Syria accepted him as the Leader of the Faithful.

Husein reckoned, however, without the Wahabi warriors of Nejd, and the mandatory interest which England and France had already established in the Near East.

On the fall of King Husein, the whole of Arabia lay at the feet of the Wahabis. The entry of Ibn Saud's troops into Mecca had, in its outward expression, increased the chances of the Wahabis for control of Arabia; or, at least, of such portions which Ibn Saud could annex. The more important result of his success was that thenceforth upon him fell the mantle of a hero who could bring about a grand federation of the men of his race. Of course, Husein's sons had been given Iraq and Transjordan as what the British liked to call 'consolation prizes', and were considered to have lost all claim to that task. The heartland of Arabia was lost to them.

The Wahabi king, long before his entry into Mecca, where he hosted the All-World Moslem Conference, had felt the call of his mission of Arab leadership.

The revival of the Ikhwan movement, which is the result of his genius, cannot be said to be of only localised interest in barren, largely nomadic Nejd. Amongst the nomads of the desert he had been infusing a Wahabi, austere religious, spirit with a zeal and skill which prepared his followers for any possible expansion.

It was no easy task for him to curb the raiding propensities of the Badu. To bring about national cohesion, peninsular Arabia had to contend with the difficulties of conflicting interests between the nomads and the settled population of the oases.

By giving fresh life to the old Wahabi tenets, he organised the Ikhwan, 'the Brothers', and founded the first of their sixty colonies at Artawiyah.

With state aid, the Ikhwan colonies of fighting tribesmen grew apace to discharge the dual function of agricultural soldiers. This system of keeping an inexpensive army, it might be said, was not unknown to the Romans.

In Arabia, however, it proved a binding factor between the settled people and the nomads. At the same time the movement served to destroy the inter-tribal competition which had been the cause of so many raids and counter-raids in the past.

Not only on account of the progress that the Wahabis have made in Arabia and the territories which they have acquired, but also owing to the hypnotic force of character of Ibn Saud, the cause of Arab consciousness was well served.

He banished many causes of tribal unrest by planting agricultural colonies in the desert where nothing grew before, and providing irrigation. He removed many of those practices of religion which, although never forming a part of the faith, had yet always served to install priestly thraldom. The directness of his character singled him out from the rest as the major leader of the Arabs.

After World War II, when most Arab peoples finally gained their independence from the European colonisers, many problems from the past continued to plague the quest for Arab unity.

These ranged from the differences of opinion which some sociologists trace to roots in the different approach to problems bequeathed by the British, the French, the Italians or the Spaniards. Then there is the fact that some Arab countries are Asian, some are African, some like to think of themselves as European. The Egyptians and Iraqis will at times hark back to their pre-Islamic past: while millions of Arabs are not Moslems at all, but Christians.

With close on two hundred million souls, with a vast mineral and agricultural wealth and an enormous land-mass extending from the Atlantic to the Indian Ocean, the Arab people will undoubtedly form one of the most important world communities of the future.

But what are its destinies, and what might be the probabilities of its attitude in regard to Europe and the rest of Asia and Africa?

13

Passion Play of Baghdad

And now what of the Fairy City of the Caliphs itself, and the kaleidoscopic changes which have embraced it since it was built?

The City of Romance was built by Caliph Mansur in 762 A.D. astride the River Tigris; its alleys are still winding and dark, its mysterious domes and minarets still rise above the rather alluring houses; the stork sits nursing its young on the edge of an overhanging bit of masonry, just as it did during the days of the Caliph Haroun al-Rashid and his Viziers.

When I say this I am speaking about the atmosphere, not of the buildings of Mansur's time, of which almost none remain. The town has died and risen again and again in history, shifting its mighty buildings, even slums, from place to place: so much so that even the site on which Mansur laid its foundation stone is disputed. Some believe it to have been where the modern railway station is now situated, others hold it to be nearer the great Shrine of Kadhimain.

But though its old glory is gone, there is still enchantment in the word *Baghdad*. The hidden courtyards, the narrow archways, intercepted here and there by the blue-tiled domes of mosques, make Baghdad a place of mystery even today.

When I was first there, walking along the only straight road called the New Street, there were open-air coffee shops, where hundreds of Bedouins, Kurdish labourers, and many town Arabs, sat sipping tea or coffee.

The Tigris crossed, and you were in the real old Baghdad; camels and donkeys carrying their loads of bricks, firewood or oil canisters.

A few of those curious round boats like coracles, peculiar to Baghdad, were approaching their moorings. Anon, from a thousand minarets the call of the evening prayer filled the air. The coffee booths were doing a brisk trade, with enormous chunks of bread being washed down by large gulps of camel's milk. Presently, the bank of the river awoke; little fires burst into existence, for the nomads, too, were preparing their first meal of the day; and so the day ended in timeless Baghdad.

But one of the greatest modern landmarks of Islamic history is undoubtedly Kadhimain, barely five miles from Baghdad.

It is the most striking city in Iraq, and that was originally due to the fact that in 802 A.D. Musa El Kadhim, the 7th Imam, a noted saint – and, incidentally, a progenitor of our family – was buried there.

Thirty years later Mohamed El-Taki, the ninth Imam, was also buried at the same place, thus giving a double sanctity to the shrine in the eyes of the faithful.

And here one sees the greatest Passion Play of Islam performed at *Ashurah* – the Tenth Day of the month of *Moharram* of the Islamic Calendar. I took an opportunity of witnessing the mournful celebration, which, to my mind, is the most spectacular scene that my eyes have ever beheld. To appreciate it to the full we need some historical background.

When the Prophet Mohamed, who preached the religion of Islam from Mecca and Medina, died in 632 A.D. – there were four likely successors to his ministry: Abu Bakr, Omar, Usman and Ali. These were called his Companions, in view of the fact that the first and the last named were his relatives, and the others had distinguished themselves in many respects for the cause of early Islam.

To the viceregency of the Prophet, they were elected in the above-mentioned order; Abu Bakr being the first Caliph, or Successor to the Leader of the Faithful.

The days of the last two of the Caliphs, namely, Usman and Ali, were stormy ones in Islamic history. Due regard must be paid to that period, because the origin of the Battle of Martyrs at Kerbela in Mesopotamia is to be found in it, and out of that battle has grown the Passion Play of the Moharram.

The cohesion of the Islamic community was maintained by Abu Bakr. His successor Omar is chiefly credited with the expansion of Islamic influence: and the inherent Arab spirit of inter-tribal war was kept in check. On the death of the Second Caliph, Omar, in 643 A.D., however, when the Third Companion Usman superseded Ali, tribal jealousies began to show themselves.

The supporters of Ali resented Usman's election on two grounds. First, Ali was the husband of Fatima, the only surviving child of the Prophet. Second, he was a close kinsman of Mohammed. And the Prophet had been devoted to his two grandsons, Hasan and Husein, children of Ali.

Ali, these people therefore claimed, had the prior claim to the leadership of Islam. They also disapproved of the appointment of one Muawiyya as governor of Syria.

This disaffection continued to smoulder for over ten years, until 655 A.D. when Usman, the Third Caliph, fell at the hand of an assassin, and Ali, the son-in-law of the Prophet, was proclaimed Caliph.

Soon after assuming the leadership of the faithful he issued orders for the recall of Muawiyya from the governorship of Syria. But the latter had by then gathered a great following, and, refusing to obey the order of the Caliph of Mecca, proclaimed himself Caliph in Damascus.

After varying moves and counter-moves on the part of each of these men, when Ali, too, fell at the hand of an assassin in 660 A.D., Muawiyya was proclaimed Caliph in northern Arabia, whilst Mecca elected Hasan, the elder of the two sons of Ali.

Both Hasan and Muawiyya disappear from the scene by 679 A.D., leaving the contest of the Caliphate to Husein, the younger brother of Hasan and Yazid, the son of Muawiyya.

The former still held Mecca, and the latter, regarding himself as the rightful monarch, challenged Husein to surrender.

The two armies faced each other on the banks of the Euphrates in what is now Iraq, where Husein was slain and his followers treated with the worst savagery in war that has ever been recorded in the history of man.

It is the dramatic portrayal of this tragedy which the mourning at Moharram has kept alive in the minds of the Moslems of the world for over thirteen centuries.

The several aspects of the battle are acted with such intensity and passion that the appeal of the drama is almost religious, especially amongst the Shia (minority) sections of the Moslems. Although it is celebrated with more or less universal vigour among the Near and the Middle Eastern people, in Persia the mourning ceremony finds its highest expression.

The reason for the Persian attachment to the Moharram Passion Play is sometimes explained by the fact that Husein, the hero and martyr of the battle, was wedded to Shahrbanu, a daughter of Yazdigird, the last Persian King of the Sasanian dynasty.

The Sharifs, known also as the Alawiya and Hashemite families, are accorded royal honours partly because of this imperial descent.

The actual period of mourning begins with the first day of the month of Moharram of the lunar calendar. The climax of this tragedy, that is, the date on which Husein was slain, being the tenth of that month, is the day of Ashurah (the tenth) when the Passion Play is performed.

During these ten days mourning is strictly observed; no marriages are celebrated then, no new thing is bought, no foundation of a home is laid. Women will wear no coloured garments, nor use cosmetics; laughter in the street, loud talking and many normal social functions are not permitted.

Gradually, as the days near the tenth of the month, the degree of public mournfulness increases. Every night meetings are held in the mosques, in the halls of wealthy citizens, even in public caravanserais. Here the Rozah Khan, a body of semi-priests who recite different versions of the Battle of Martyrs, sing melodiously and pathetically of the day on which the Prophet's grandson was killed at Kufa.

To the Shiahs, attendance at these gatherings ranks equally with prayer-meetings.

Usually at the close of the afternoon prayer, but often at night, hundreds are trekking to their illuminated mosque.

When Moharram falls in the winter, the rich come clad

in their big fur coats, the poor wrapped in coarse home-spun. They come slish-slushing, walking, tumbling, wading through the snow in the winding streets.

Women move in droves, holding on to their babies or the voluminous cloaks around them. They have often heard the sad tale of Mohamed's family being done to death so cruelly; and yet they are willing and earnest listeners as they sit, row upon row, before the speakers. Women are already sobbing; one of the over-faithful is visibly affected; tears are running down his beard.

At last the Reciter of Poems mounts the pulpit.

'It is a strange story,' he says amidst intense silence. 'Aye! It is a sad and lamentable commentary upon valour and devolution that warriors of such blue blood as Husein were slain!'

The whole gathering bursts out in a chorus of loud weeping and wailing. 'Aye! Aye!' they shriek through their tears.

'It was cruel, that fate which befell the bone and blood of the Holy Prophet himself!' and they cry on.

'It is time,' again says the reciter, raising his voice above the general din, 'it is time to listen and to shed tears of blood for the tragedy of Husein.'

He sings, he recites, he is depicting the way in which the slayer of Husein drew his sword; now he sits, showing how the Martyr tried to extract the arrow from the throat of his infant son; now again the reciter throws his handkerchief over his turban, and acts the part of Zobeida, the sister of the Martyr; and then unveiling himself, signifies the agony of the lady when she finds that the thirst of the infants was being assuaged only by the tears of women, as the enemy would not give them a single drop of water.

The mastery of imagination with which these scenes are depicted, aided by allegory and appeal to passion such as can perhaps only be found in the Persian language, are all unsurpassed by the skill of these reciters. Not a single person in the whole gathering is in a composed state of mind.

Some have already fainted through beating upon their breasts; others have utterly exhausted themselves with wailing. There are red rings around their tear-stained eyes. And yet, at every additional recitation, they continue to wail loud and long, men's hoarse weeping and coughing blending with the shrill lamentations of women.

At each pause the whole house rocks with unbelievably intense emotion, and when they are thus oblivious of everything, the priest has left his place, and they hardly notice. But it is well past the midnight hour and all trek home to snatch what little sleep they can, only to rise to another day of mourning. And thus these side-shows, so to speak, of the great Passion Play go on from day to day until the night of the tenth of Moharram, when during the morning of that day, the Play is acted in its full pageantry, thus bringing to a close one of the finest examples of Eastern Passion Dramas.

The tenth and the last day of mourning dawns upon Shiahs and Sunnis alike in Asia with the gloom of the occasion, for the great procession takes place this day.

Practically every person, male and female, takes part. Every shop in the town is closed, and thousands have already betaken themselves to sit at the wayside where the procession is to pass. The more devout and able-bodied men, having stripped themselves to the waist, stand before the portable wooden structure representing the bier of Husein the Martyr, in their district of the town.

At about nine in the morning the *Tazias*, the above-mentioned wooden biers, are seen making the round of the city. From their different localities they converge on the principal square of the town, from whence they are to proceed towards the last resting place of the biers. All along the route, additional men swell the number of those who are carrying the several Tazias to the central meeting-place; in aggregate, they might well exceed thirty thousand men.

Every hundred yards or more is a station for the procession, poems of lamentation are recited, men beat upon their breasts, women watching from the balconies take up the wailing and are left crying as the Tazia moves on.

Here and there, especially in India, youths may engage in fencing and sword-dances, representing the soldiers of the Martyr; and at wayside booths sherbet or water is distributed free to the people, an act which carries much religious merit in the play. One of its most harrowing scenes is when the innocent family and followers of the Martyr were denied water by their foes at the battle of Kerbela.

A little before noon the Tazias from different localities enter the main square of the town. The crowd has increased enormously. Soon, the thud-thudding of small drums is heard, various stations where the biers are to be deposited are cleared, and a passage is made for the chief procession.

First come some half-a-dozen boys clad in black, thumping small drums; they are followed by men bearing banners depicting the arms of the Martyr; and now a band of big men stripped to the waist, with spiked chains, thorns and heavy horseshoes hanging around their necks, their heads shaven, are beating upon their bare chests with chains.

Blood is often seen to gush out with each blow as they raise their hands in unison and call in loud chorus: 'Hasan, Husein; Hasan, Husein,' the names of the two sons of Ali.

This is followed by a number of camels and mules representing the pack animals of the Martyr's camp. A hundred horses bedecked in fine shawl pieces, and others led by their riders, pass next in the procession. After that come thirty-five camel riders who represent the female, infant and aged members of Husein's family; then representations of the seventy-two bodies of those slain at the battle; and seven heads on lances, escorted by horsemen. The heads on lance-points are represented by large lemons. The horse of the Chief Martyr is led at this end of the procession, and last of all comes Hazrat Abbas, the standard-bearer, with eighty water-carriers.

The passion of the mourners is at its highest at this juncture. Men form into small groups. At a given signal, a sea of arms shoots up in the air and descends upon their bared chests with a thud that can be heard like waves on a distant shore. Again and again the arms rise, and with increasing force and frequency, breasts are beaten and women wail.

'What happened to Husein?' one asks.

'Husein became a martyr!' reply a thousand voices in unison, and then the arms rise high in the air, now descending on their shaven heads, then on their breasts; and so it goes on till dusk.

As a result of excitement and exposure, fatal casualties are not infrequently reported after this Passion Play. For weeks afterwards, hospitals are full of people suffering from pneumonia and self-inflicted wounds, but as the drama has acquired a religious flavour, the ill-effects of the performance are cheerfully borne; indeed, are often courted.

It is obvious therefore that, without the exhibition of such extraordinary spectacles, fervour for the only Passion

Play of Islam could not have been kept at white heat for over a thousand years to this day.

You cannot fully savour this description without comparing it to other Passion Plays of the East, for only thus can I give you an inkling of the difference between the minds of Arabs and other Easterners.

This Moslem drama, as we have seen, has assumed almost a religious status. Its counterpart is to be found in the Hindu epic of the *Ramayana*, the story of which was laid down many centuries before the Christian era. One of the greatest of the Passion Plays of Hindu India is *Ram Lilla*, the recounting of the exploits and hardships of Prince Rama as described in the Ramayana.

The poetical genius both of the author of Ramayana and of Firdousi of Persia, true to the Eastern turn of mind, exalted a national hero into divinity – or at least to the status of local saintship: Rama, Rustam and Sohrab. In like manner, many lesser singers of India have created other characters for Passion Plays. Thus, for instance, we have *The Actions of Chaityanna* about the seventh century; *The Life of Sankaracharya*, ninth century; down to such recent dates as the eighteenth century depicting the life work and trials of Siraj ad-Dawla. But none have captured the imagination of the people as firmly as the episodes of the hero of Ramayana, as shown in Ram Lilla.

In understanding this Hindu play, the difference between it and the Passion Drama of Moharram must be borne in mind. Both strive to appeal to the most profound, the most intense of human feelings – there is the same effort to glorify the young hero, struggling as he is against overwhelming odds, the same depicting of battle scenes, the same lesson of 'truth triumphant'. But of the two, as a play Ram Lilla is the more complete: it finishes the story.

In the lamentation ceremony of Moharram your grief is

so intensified that it almost surges above rationality, so that after you have heard of the atrocities of the battle of Kerbela and are hysterical with emotion: faced with the army of Yazid, you would fling yourself upon it in battle.

Not so the Ram Lilla, for the story tells you how the beloved Crown Prince Rama is banished to the jungle for fourteen years with his wife Sita; how his younger brother refuses to rule, but places Rama's shoes on the throne and 'sitting under their shadow, he rules in the name of Rama till he returns', after his vow of fourteen years of exile is fulfilled; how during this period of exile, Sita is kidnapped by the 'Bad King' of Ceylon, and how Rama aided by Hanuman, the Monkey General, invades Ceylon, slays Rawan, the Bad King, rescues Sita and lives happily ever after, so to speak.

All these scenes are more-or-less grotesquely acted out on open air-stages in Indian cities. Youths representing Rama and his wife Sita dressed in the early garb of the Hindus parade the streets, heading a procession and followed by drum-beaters and brass bands. Later, they are shown to take leave of their subjects as they disappear into a mango grove, as if to exile. The battle scene is depicted by hordes of men striking upon each other's drums and war dances take place, marking the conquest of Ceylon. Some men use masks of monkey faces, thus forming the legions of the Monkey General who helped Rama against Rawan. The Princess Sita is then tested for her chastity by 'walking through a blaze of fire'. When she proves the integrity of her honour whilst in Rawan's captivity, boys sing her praises and conches are blown mightily. Food is distributed to the performers; and finally the entire concourse of humanity follow Rama to an adjoining clearing in the jungle, where an enormous effigy of Rawan is erected, and Rama sets light to it. Whilst it burns, the people sing, boys dance and players stand in the glow of the crackling fire of burning Rawan until its ashes can be taken home to make potions for curing all sorts of diseases, from a sore eye to malarial fever.

In the extensive land area stretching from Eastern Bengal to China, one sees dramatic performances which are acted within the precincts of local deities. According to informed belief, these were once living personalities, and by their beneficence to the people or by some outstanding exploits in war, were exalted to the status of saints or even gods. But it is generally contended that in the countries of East Asia, barring China and Japan, much of the drama falls into the category of spirit worship. It is, however, in China that we meet with examples of true Passion Plays.

Even during the time of Confucius in 500 B.C., ritualistic dramas were performed at which wands and battleaxes were brandished by actors. This clearly shows that the Passion Plays of the Chinese must have originated as war plays, or at least arise out of the general human propensity to exalt and to honour the heroes of war. That such dramas cannot have a lasting hold upon the people without a goodly admixture of religious thought is evinced by the fact that in the Chinese plays, as in those of the Moslems and the Hindus, the pious association with the 'holiness of these war adventures' was introduced. Thus, no-one in Persia considers the Moharram events as merely the Battle of Kerbela, any more than the invasion of Rama is regarded as being only to rescue his wife Sita. Nor, indeed, is it the case with the career of Kuan Ti, the God of War, who, during the period of the Chinese romantic chivalry of 220 A.D., took a noble part in the Wars of the Three Kingdoms. Thus the heroes of these three plays, although human, were ranked with the other saints of the several religions.

In such a drama as the God of War, the performers are, as a rule, drawn from the professional acting class, the company often consisting of sixty men. No women are allowed to appear, their parts being played by men. Unlike the Indians and the Japanese they use no masks, but artificial hair is often used to indicate the growth of beard. Quite in keeping with their national love of thoroughness, an actor sometimes has to memorise between one hundred and two hundred parts, in addition to undergoing vigorous training in acrobatics and acquiring a very thorough knowledge of the historical background of the play.

An open-air stage is generally used for such a passion play. A large thatched pavilion is erected in an open field, and plants are placed on the terraced ground prepared as seating accommodation for the spectators. The stage should face a shrine, so that the gods themselves may have a view of the performance.

From early morning, crowds start to gather at the theatre; precisely at noon the play begins, and it goes on until sunset. There is no curtain, the stage being merely a raised platform with no scenic effects behind it.

Presently a character appears, and silence falls. He tells the audience whom he is representing. Then the orchestra begins to play, attendants stand in readiness with chairs, tables or even screens to bring up to the stage when the actor wants them to make his piece the more realistic. Another comes to play his part, and then another; they sing, they dance, they show their skill at fencing, and it is not unusual to see water or tea handed up to an actor during the performance. As there is no dropping of the curtain at the close of an act, all the characters stand and then walk quickly around the stage in single file. A clash of cymbals brings the play to an end and thus, the story of the

God of War continues to live in the hearts of the Chinese, as do the exploits of Husein in Persia, and of Rama or Krishna in Hindustan: for these Passion Plays of Asia have a deep-rooted association with the living religions of the East.

14

Pink Rose of the Hills

After Baghdad, I bent my steps westward, for I had to reach Damascus, from where I intended to journey back to the interior of Syria.

I had not progressed far when at Hit I beheld a fascinating Arab ceremony – the Eid or Bairam festival. It is staged in much the same manner as they celebrate it in the great square facing the citadel of Aleppo.

Thousands of Bedouins trek to the city for the sword-dance contest, when experts from each tribe leap into the arena and contest their skill in swordsmanship. They whirl themselves about, uttering war-whoops and slashing the empty air with their glittering blades. The real skill is contained in both attacking and defending oneself with the sword, for no shields are used.

When this is over, small groups of men dance round and round a camel, holding their arms aloft, while others keep time by clapping their hands. The same kind of dance is seen during an Arab procession which goes to Nabi Musa, near Jerusalem, to celebrate the birth of Moses. The crowd becomes very thick towards the late afternoon when there is a short dance for the entertainment of women.

Veiled women sit concealed behind the latticed

balconies of the houses that surround the square in front of the citadel. A small procession of boys, ranging from eight to twelve, approaches the gathering and takes its stand in the centre of the ring. Big drums are beaten mightily, a chant is taken up by the crowd as a veiled performer, riding a camel, is seen to emerge from the cloistered bazaars.

Slowly the camel, on which heavy and expensive rugs are thrown, wends its way through the crowd. The rider, though really a man, is dressed in women's clothes, and the dress is that of a bride.

When the camel has reached the centre of the space, the boys form a ring around it; the music swells mightily in volume, and every throat is working overtime.

Then the performer balances herself on her knees, her face still veiled; and throws her arms up, then twists and bends her form to the tune of the music. Next she stands up on the back of the camel and dances with more dignity.

This is considered to be the 'spirit of youth' expressed by the newly-wed. Presently, a slower chant is heard, the performer unveils herself and repeats the previous dance, sitting on her knees on the back of the camel. The un-veiling expresses her wedded life. Finally the rhythm of the music slows, symbolising the coming of a woman's later years, with which the performance terminates. In the real sense of the word, these may be called the folk-dances of the northern tribes of Arabia.

At the caravanserai at Hit, I chanced to meet a man whose troubles were the same as mine: neither of us could afford the time to linger in the desert, but for long, we could find no means of transport faster than a camel.

Yusuf Khan was not an Arab. His one desire was to go

on a pilgrimage to Mecca, as his days were growing short. As he put it, speaking of his white hair: 'The snow on the mountains is a sign of the approach of evening'.

Together with his wife, he had travelled thus far from the snow peaks of Gilgit. A great Khan, a chieftain, too, was he of his mighty clan that 'could challenge the power of all the Mehtars of Chitral'. But, now he had renounced the world and all it meant. Having already bent his head at such shrines as those of Mashshad, in Afghanistan and in Iraq, Najaf and Karbala, he was bound for Jerusalem and thence to Holy Mecca, where he hoped to end his days.

Though old in years and a pilgrim, Yusuf Khan still retained the old fire of a chieftain in his eyes. He chose that Iraqi road to reach Jerusalem on purpose, to visit the shrines in order, the holiest last. He did not want to tarry in a desert serai a day longer and miss his chance of the season of the pilgrimage at the Mosque of the Kaaba at Mecca.

So a camel caravan was no good to him. He must get a motor-car. Even a second-hand Ford would do; and that car he bought at the price of a new one; for money now mattered naught to Yusuf, the frontier chieftain who had abandoned the world.

In this car, he also gave me a lift to Damascus, and during the weary miles of travel westward, he told me his story.

Yusuf Khan was a warrior by birth, ancestry, tradition and inclination. There were those who called him a brigand, but then one was bound to hear such jealousies when outstanding deeds of bravery like those of the handsome Yusuf Khan were mentioned.

All the valley of the Khyber: and Badakhshan, and

Kafiristan, rang with his praises. His name was in the mouth of everyone and none cared to disagree with him, for as they said when discussing him – which they only did in quiet tones when there was no sign of a boulder large enough to hide a man – he fought like Shaitan the Stoned himself.

'Yusuf Khan will take thee', was all that needed to be said to the most disobedient child, to have it show the desired cooperation.

Now, like all warriors, Yusuf Khan was vulnerable. That weakness was found by Halima, the only daughter of a neighbouring chieftain.

The last time the warrior had been on a little private business trip – transborder unofficial commerce, it was called in those parts – which had taken him to the chieftain's fort, he had seen a vision of loveliness: a perfect *houri* in a setting of pink roses. This for sure was the lovely Halima, of whom his little sister Ayesha had often spoken.

Strictly speaking, Yusuf Khan, warrior or no, should not have looked, or if by mistake his eyes had alighted, the look should not have been repeated.

The etiquette of the clans forbade it to the extent of killing the offender; so great was the disgrace that it became an insult, and in Pashtun frontier law, an insult can only be wiped out by blood. And that blood was not the childish scratching we know in the West as providing satisfaction. That blood was the blood of death.

They are more than sticklers for correct behaviour where their honour is concerned, these highlanders. Yusuf Khan was a man of honour, as becomes a warrior, and so he looked away, torn as was his heart by the sight. But, just as he did so, a rose, pink and enchanting, fell at his feet. Now what would any warrior do under the circumstances? Precisely what Yusuf Khan did: pick it up.

This was the very shaft of love itself, he thought, as he raised the scented perfection to his lips, while his eyes, heedless even of blood-feuds, sought the wall of the garden behind which the most perfect rose in the world bloomed.

Only the bare ramparts met his gaze. Had it been a dream? No, it could not have been; the rose remained. The blood rushed to the warrior's head, his senses swam, the sight of so much beauty had conquered him as no strong arm could have done.

What had he done? This could mean real trouble. Had anyone seen him? Anyone even now unsheathing his long sword to fight to the death? Yusuf Khan was no coward. He had looked too often straight into the grisly face of death and – laughed. But there was no sense in courting danger.

Hastily he tucked the rose in his tunic. What right had a man of the sword with roses? And yet! Yes, assuredly Yusuf Khan, the warrior, whom some called brigand, and all feared, had his weak moments.

Quickly he turned away and went to the Durbar, the room in which he would be sure to find the old chieftain holding court; and perhaps his sons, Yusuf's own friends.

They were there, in full durbar.

'Peace upon you,' Yusuf Khan greeted them.

'And upon you peace,' chorussed the men.

'The very man we want, my sons! Here as though the message, as yet only in these heads of ours, had reached him by the magic of a genie!'

'I am honoured to be even thought of by you, Khan Sahib. Whatever you require of me will be given freely. My head, eyes and heart are at your service.'

Yusuf Khan had never felt that he needed bravery before. What had happened to him? He shook like a moneylender faced by a warrior on a lonely road. Never had he felt fear: not even that time when his horse had been cut down under him and he had had to fight four armed men single-handed.

But then he had never experienced these new emotions; emotions that make cowards of the bravest.

He waited for the bombshell to burst about his head. The chief was sure to perceive his pounding head, his racing heart, and know the truth.

What was this he had done? He would be declared an immoral interloper, an enemy. He would have to fight back... How could he raise his hand in war against his dearest friends? What would his father say?

Terrible thought! Surely his father would kill him without a moment's thought. A fine end for a warrior!

The old chieftain had fallen into a reverie; the sons looked sideways at each other: only the hubble-bubble of the tobacco smoke passing through the water-pipe broke the silence.

At length the visitor, not feeling able to bear it longer, raised his eyes from the ground to the face of the chieftain. What he saw there was not encouraging. The hookah was neglected. Sullen anger spread over the rugged features. Hate had screwed the eyes up, until they had almost disappeared. Truly a terrible countenance!

Terrible even to a man who had expected it. To one who deserved it, and knew he deserved it? The young man trembled anew, for the silence was worse to him than the heat of battle and the clashing of Khyber knives.

'Yusuf Khan,' the voice held in check but little, broke the silence at last, like thunder it was, thunder in the dead of night. The old eyes flashed like lightning over the Khyber peaks.

'Thy father is mine best friend. Thy mother was mine

172

sister. Side by side have we stood in many a battle thou canst yet hear tell of in the Peshawar Story-Tellers bazaar. For forty years have we been as brothers. Only today has mine house been insulted, and old man as I am, this fair right hand of mine shall defend mine honour while I yet breathe.'

Again silence fell.

The hand of Yusuf Khan who had never known fear, shook as it strayed to that part of his tunic under which lay the scented emblem of his thoughtless action. It strengthened him.

The old chieftain raised his head defiantly to gaze upon Yusuf Khan as he said: 'My youngest sister's son has this day been slain by Akbar Ali, with whom, as everyone knows, they have a blood feud. That nephew of mine was as my own son, and now he is dead. Wai...e! Wai...e!'

The open-mouthed look of amazement which overspread the face of the visitor was totally out of proportion to the effect the news had upon him. He had never even liked the nephew, his cousin: who was now, in death, stretching out a hand to help him – almost the hand of friendship. For Yusuf saw an opportunity.

Yusuf Khan had not, however, yet quite recovered from his astonishment. His tongue clove to the roof of his mouth, his ears burned. He could only continue his incredulous stare.

'Thou, the son of my best friend, may well be beyond speech – but fear not: for we shall wipe out the family of this viper, with the help of Allah, May His Name be Exalted!

'Go thou, to thy father, give him my salaam. Tell him the story, the rest I leave to him. If I know my best friend as well as I think, there will be support to hearten me on this raid of raids!'

'The message shall be delivered to my father with the utmost speed.' Yusuf bowed, hand on heart.

'This enemy of ours is a man of great strength, armed with the modern rifles of the Farangi soldiers. Strong are they as the young of the lion, and as bold,' went on the chieftain.

'Strong and bold are we, too, O Khan Sahib,' said the visitor, 'and none can afford not to know of our bravery.'

The old chieftain looked admiringly at Yusuf Khan's six-feet-three of strong muscle and litheness, the agility of a tiger, and looking he took heart.

'This raid shall see the end of my foe and by the hoof of the Evil One, anything thou carest to ask for shall be thine, Yusuf Khan, when we are victorious! Be ready tomorrow night. Now go, tell thy father, and God be your Protector.'

In a fever of excitement, the warrior jumped into the saddle and clattered out on to the road. It was a good twenty miles home, but no horseman ever had more cheering words ringing in his ears than the promise the Khan had given. 'Anything thou carest to ask for shall be thine.'

The very thudding of the horses' hoofs was a song of love! Once he startled an Indian itinerant grocer by galloping almost into him. The mild Hindu held up his hands, ready, as usual in these violent parts, to plead for his life and to disclaim extortionate habits: but Yusuf Khan only laughed loudly and galloped recklessly on, leaving the Hindu thanking whichever god he could think of first in his amazement.

There had been a time when the hillman would have enjoyed a little amusement at the expense of the money-lender, but this was no ordinary day – this was the greatest day of his life, and Yusuf Khan galloped on, singing the lilting Pashtun song about the love of the Bulbul, the nightingale, for the rose. It was a new role for the warrior to fill, that of a Bulbul!

Within two hours he reached home. Steam rose from his sweating and foam-splashed horse. This non-stop race was no new thing for the Arab mare, who had as little fear of whizzing bullets as did her master.

A few minutes and the story was told to his father.

'Of a truth I will stand by mine old friend, even though these enemy sons of a pig shall be armed with Farangi rifles, yet will I trust to Allah, and the old turn of my wrist; when do we attack?'

'Khan Sahib awaits your reply.'

'Even now shall I send it and tomorrow while yet the insult tastes bitterest in our mouths, dusk shall witness our preparedness. Send a servant with this reply now.'

Yusuf Khan thought jealously of the rifles. What chance had his old father, even with the far-famed wrist-play of his sword against those sons of Shaitan, armed with guns stolen from the Farangi army?

Ah! There was an idea! There was music to the soul! Perhaps even a little music of the sword on this, the greatest day in his life. A raid on the Franks' camp! What others had done, of a truth he, Yusuf Khan, would do.

He thought quickly. No meditation for the warrior! Prayer and meditation for the weak! The high-road and the knife for the warrior. The high-road it would be and the knife only if necessity called. Yusuf Khan liked the call of necessity.

It was a long road, and bold, quick work would have to be done before the rifles could be filched from the Farangi barracks. Even nerves of steel would be sorely tried. The warrior was not a stranger to these tactics. There was that little affair with the soldiers at Kohat, another at Landi Kotal. Fine and full of adventure had those skirmishes been! Moreover, what were the Farangi soldiers doing there if they were not intended to fight? They were not exactly in their own country, were they? Supposedly they came to fight: very well, give them a fight. And what was more exciting than a small engagement on an impulse, so to speak? Truly these delicate affairs made life the glad thing it was!

Nothing must be left to chance. Had the two brown eyes made a coward of the warrior, whom some called brigand, and who had never thought of chance before? For whom the knife had ever been sufficient unto the day? Never had he realised how dear life was. He must not die yet, with so much to live for! He touched the rose again. That would be his mascot. With this he would brave a whole nation, a world full of Farangis, and conquer! That rose alone, not even the Hand of Fatima, the good-luck charm which his mother had hung round his neck when he was a boy, would come before it.

Yusuf Khan thought out his campaign as he set out for the heights above the British infantry fort. Through the rough hills he went and through these by the mercy of Allah he would retrace his steps with the rifles, lest anyone met him on the road. The road was not the place for anyone trying to hide anything.

Ah, there was the place, just behind that boulder! Home, said they, of the greatest warriors of Inglistan. Very well. In Thy Name, All-Highest!

Creeping on all fours, the hillman got behind the great stone. Warily, with the ease of the practised scout, he peered round the rocky side and took in the plan of the Farangi camp.

The sun glanced again and again on the rifle the sentry carried on his march backwards and forwards. Fifty paces he took, then turned, made a few fancy steps in turning and then paced fifty back. Not much of a life for a man, even a Farangi one, thought Yusuf Khan, this pacing backwards and forwards; nothing like the open hills and perhaps the possession of the one who had thrown the rose, one who already thought favourably of him. A haze even as pink as the rose itself floated round the warrior as he lay waiting for nightfall.

What thoughts passed through his mind during those hours! What thought did not! How many times did he attack the Farangi army in different ways, finally marching in with all his clan, to the annihilation of the foe!

At long last, the time had come. Yusuf Khan had been cramped for so long, he felt stiff all over. First he exercised his limbs, to get the stiffness out of them. Then he crept slowly, lest any dislodged stone betray him.

Down, down he went laboriously, without a sound. The jagged edges of the stones tore his hands. The cutting of the tough barbed wire blistered them, already pierced and bleeding. He stopped every now and again to listen. Strange, how perfect is the hearing of the hillman. Nothing! Crawling through the cut barbed wire which tore his clothes, face and limbs, he was finally behind the fort wall. Still the monotonous sound of the sentry, who was probably visualising what he would do when, his service over, he returned home.

Once over that wall, there will be some pretty work, thought Yusuf Khan. The sentry started on his walk back. The warrior was over! Like a panther he crept in the shadow of the wall – to his amazement he saw, not a dozen feet away, a stack of brand-new short-magazine Lee-Enfield rifles, dull in their camouflage paint, with cartridge belts beside them. There was no time to be lost.

It would be a pity to stab a man in the back, but only stunned he might recover and the rifles would be lost. The rifles that would make another chapter of history in the Khyber! He must kill.

It was the work of a few seconds. The long Khyber knife glittered and fell, the sentry slumped to the earth without a sound and mercifully, even his rifle made no noise.

Huh! There was no fight in these eaters of pig's flesh! No wonder they invented instruments for killing at a distance.

A few more seconds and four rifles and cartridge-belts were over the shoulders of the warrior – who did not notice the weight in the excitement of the capture. Here, within his grasp, were the weapons to exterminate every foe on two legs! The weapons to unlock the door to his Paradise! – for, within the next twenty-four hours, the enemies of the house of his beloved would be dead, dead as the Farangi sentry.

Back he laboured, through the barbed wire entanglement. Suddenly he turned; what was that noise? The dead sentry had been found!

Commands! Rifles spat bullets all round, but Yusuf Khan was out of reach of the blind firing. He hurried up the difficult hill in the darkness, the pace hard even for a man who had spent hours memorising the way. On he went, sure-footed as a hill goat, now well out of reach of any pursuers who would never be foolish enough to follow up those heights, even though they knew where he was. This was Pashtun sniper country: and the highlanders owned it, whatever the Franks might say.

That was better! He would rest now, and hide the guns under his voluminous fur posteen. The cartridge belts he would carry around his massive frame.

It was an easy matter now to get home and tell the good news. The Farangis would make a fuss over the dead sentry. They called themselves soldiers, but made trouble if one was killed. Were there no Farangis who cared to die the death of a warrior? Pah! They'd show their cowardice by bombing some unprotected villages, that was all. This would enable the women to bring up their sons to know what manner of people these Inglis really were! And Yusuf Khan forcefully cleared his throat, and spat.

'We shall even make them eat the dust before us,' said his father, fingering the Lee-Enfields lovingly. 'What a raid this promises to be!' laughed the old man wickedly and gleefully in his throat, as though already in the thick of it.

That night, just as the old chieftain and his friends had collected for the attack, a forward scout arrived breathlessly to say that the enemy was converging on the fort from the south.

Rushing to the tower, the chieftain took up his accustomed position. The others manned the loopholes. Thus they had the advantage of the unsuspecting raiders, who were allowed to crawl up to the walls to be shot at close range. But the house of Akbar Ali had not been established through its members running away. Several fell with their faces to the foe.

The others rushed the walls, zig-zagging and firing as they ran. Some got over the wall, attacking the defenders like enraged tigers. They were brave men who could defeat Akbar Ali and he knew it. The fighting became too close for rifles. No word was spoken; grappling with stabbing, flashing knives, death-dealing smashes, guttural gasps – every second was tense.

The father of Yusuf Khan forgot his age: he was again the warrior of old, face to face with the enemy. Here was the position he had always loved. Yusuf Khan remembered the rose and laughed. The followers fought for the honour of their clan and gloated over possible plunder, while in her room a young girl prayed.

The left arm of Yusuf Khan was useless, but the right still continued the good work. Here attacking him was the raiding chieftain himself – Yusuf Khan jumped on him and the two fell and rolled on the ground. When one arm is useless, double work has to be done by the other, that is all. More than double was being done now by the right hand of Yusuf Khan. The chieftain was now disarmed.

'Hast made thy peace with Allah, scoundrel of the black heart! Murderer of my brother! Take a last good look at Yusuf Khan; on this my lucky day it is fitting thou shouldst see me last!' The chief lay on his back, pierced through the heart.

'Praise be to Allah, the Merciful, the Compassionate,' said the warrior with fervour.

Yusuf Khan, blinded with blood from a gash over his right eye, staggered against the wall. Only four men stood. His father was not one of them. The famous twist of the hand had at last failed the old raider.

At last, making his way painfully to the tower, Yusuf Khan's shoulders were grasped by the old chieftain. His grief at the loss of his old friend was great.

'Wai...e! Wai...e! That I should gaze on the face of thee in death, O my brother!' he wailed.

Yusuf Khan was weak from loss of blood. He grieved not for his father who had died as he wished. Died with the shout of victory in his throat! Not for him slow death beneath the quilt, he had always said. It was the Will of Allah.

The wounds were bandaged and the men gathered to talk over the fight.

'What wilt thou claim, O son of a great father?' asked the chieftain of Yusuf Khan.

'Tomorrow, Aga, I shall present myself and tell thee.'

'It is good; then I shall await thee, for on mine honour thou didst fight even as thy father did at thine age.'

Yusuf Khan was now chieftain in his father's place. Chief of as brave a band of men as one could find in the length and breadth of the Frontier! He would be more acceptable to the chieftain as the husband of Brown Eyes. The rose had faded as is the way of even the pinkest rose, but the dry petals represented all that was beautiful to the eyes and imagination of the warrior. Look at the luck it had brought him in the Farangis' camp! Luck again in the raid! With his own sharpened sword he had killed the enemy chieftain. What more did a fighting man ask?

Only now the bride to claim! He would settle down and be at peace. Fighting and raiding were not easy for married men, at least, not so easy. Yusuf Khan did not want to commit himself; after all, he was a warrior first and a warrior chieftain at that! Still, he would cultivate fruit trees, apricots and mulberries, and yes! a rose garden wherein the delight of his heart could roam. Together they would live at peace with their neighbours – and – love!

It was not the next day, nor for many days, that Yusuf Khan set off for the chieftain's fort. His arm had given him a good deal of pain and he was obliged to give it time to heal.

At length one day, dressed in his best clothes, he visited the chieftain and asked permission to speak to him alone.

'I have come for what thou didst promise me, O Khan!' said Yusuf Khan, with his eyes on the ground.

'Speak, my son, it is thine.'

'I want to marry thy daughter Halima!'

Fury convulsed the face of the old man.

'Anything thou canst have, save my only daughter. Have my land, my crops, horses . . .'

'No, Khan Sahib, I claim thy daughter. Thou art a man of honour and made no exclusions. Thy daughter or nothing.'

'Knowest thou, young man, that I have had many feuds over the same question? Thou knowest well,' the old man shook with passion, 'the beginning of the feud which cost thy honoured father his life was started thuswise.'

'I care not, and I swear now, in thy presence, none other shall wed her, but I shall kill with these mine hands.'

As Yusuf Khan stood before him erect, with blazing eyes, the old chieftain calmed down, for he now felt instinctively that here was a fitting mate even for his daughter. He would prove still further the worth of this would-be son-in-law.

'There are many would wed this mine daughter, and I propose to hold open sports, shooting, sword-dancing, tent-pegging, etc., and the winner of all the events can claim my daughter as the prize.'

'It is well, Khan Sahib, she is mine, for no right arm can match this one of mine own.'

'A week from today then, gather all the gallants in the courtyard and prove thy mettle. Until then, adieu.'

Out walked the old chief and after him followed Yusuf Khan. The wall of the rose garden was deserted and his heart was sad. He was not expected to see a lovely face, also sad, gazing after him through the narrow confines of a latticed window.

Nevertheless, he feared as only lovers can fear for his beloved. He was also not expected to know that the chieftain was fully aware that none could defeat Yusuf Khan, and that he wanted to have an opportunity of showing the prowess of his future son-in-law.

Yusuf Khan went home. What a long time must be before it was a week to the day! The warrior experienced more doubts and fears in that week than most men do in a lifetime. Suppose! he kept asking himself, only to be answered by 'if?'. He would surely die of anguish before the time, he who had lain in wait weeks for an enemy and thought naught of it! And when the enemy did appear he was not alone, and yet Yusuf Khan alone was left after the engagement.

These were the things that proved whether a man was a warrior or a cheese! Yet here he was reduced to fear and trembling when he thought of a girl! Gazing on a few withered rose-leaves and seeing two appealing brown eyes through a bower of pink roses! Verily that which had come over him was of a peculiar nature! Not even felt the night he raided the Farangi arms! His mare stood unexercised in her stable, until his friends pestered him to take her out. His hates were forgotten. Thus the week passed and Yusuf Khan awoke one morning, *the* morning! Such a morning as to make the warrior notice a bird singing to its mate in the garden. A strange thing for a man of the sword to heed, especially when that man was Yusuf Khan!

The warrior was early in the saddle and the first to arrive. A good omen! Presently, the courtyard was filled and the events began.

The first was shooting from bare-backed galloping horses. All men were equally good shots, all after Yusuf Khan. The wrestling was watched with utmost attention. These young Adonises of the Frontier were all muscle and determination, but all, again, came after Yusuf Khan. Sword-dancing but proved to be as his hobby. All gathered closely round in a ring to watch the supple youth who leaped so swiftly and accurately round and over the blades. It was a sight to gladden the hearts of even an enemy.

The applause resounded through the courtyard. Now

refreshments were to be given out and an hour's rest for
the entrants.

Yusuf Khan went to collect his coat which he had flung
over the farther wall of the courtyard. Drawing it on, he
noticed a figure standing in the shadow of a doorway. The
woman wore an all-enveloping burqa, and so her face was
hidden. Yusuf Khan had to pass her on the way to the
food. With eyes on the ground, he came opposite to the
doorway.

'I would speak with thee,' said the voice of a woman
from the folds of the veil. Taking a sweeping look, she
crossed quickly to the other side to where the man stood.
'My mistress sends me and bids me give thee this.' She
held out a rose, a pink rose.

'Who is thy mistress?'

'I dare not say. But, surely, I do not have to say? Thou
knowest if I am found talking to thee I may suffer death.'

'Go, woman, tarry not in such danger. Give my salute to
thy mistress and tell her . . .' but just then a footstep
sounded. The woman slunk away and Yusuf Khan heard
his name called. He had been missed and the refreshments
were quickly disappearing. He tucked the rose into his
tunic and joined the company.

Yusuf Khan trod on air. Who could the sender of the
pink rose be but the chieftain's daughter? The warrior sat
down with the rest, adjusted his turban and raised his eyes
to where the latticed veranda proclaimed the women's
apartments. Only for a second did he allow his eyes to
dwell on that spot; then he sat silent amid the chattering
throng.

'Yusuf Khan,' teased one of his friends, 'such tame
work as this is not for thee, for thou hast lost thy speech! It
takes a raid to make thee talk.'

'Perhaps thou art right, Dawud Jan,' replied the silent

184

one, while the joke became general and everybody laughed.

'See,' called another, 'our brother even blushes.'

'Fool,' cried the now-enraged Yusuf Khan, 'let us fight, so that we prove who is the better man.'

Yusuf Khan was tearing off his coat just as he remembered the pink rose. The company would like nothing better than to see a rose fall from the coat of the great warrior! He could imagine how the walls would echo their laughter. To be mocked at on this day of all days!

'What is this, Dawud Jan?' inquired the chieftain. 'Art so jealous of the winner thou must run the chance of such a beating as thou hast never had? Yusuf Khan dared not begin to strike thee. Run and see where the servant has gone who was to bring the sherbet!'

Thus was the shame of Yusuf Khan averted.

At the end of the day he was the winner, and after the guests had gone home, the pact was sealed between the old chieftain and the young one, and such a marriage ceremony as theirs was, had never been seen before nor since in the whole Frontier.

'And did the chieftain give up raiding, Khan Sahib?' I inquired.

For a moment he did not speak, then turning to his wife who sat beside him he said: 'Did I, my pink Rose?'

She laughed so happily and contentedly, this old and once beautiful woman, that I knew he had grown the fruit trees and the rose garden – more especially the latter – and I thought as I looked at this fine old chieftain that none who knew and feared him in the days when he was the far-famed warrior some called brigand, would have recognised him. The rose had proved mightier than the sword.

15

Golden Dawns of Syria

Men were loitering in groups around the Government Offices – the schoolboys were playing truant with an obvious zest – the women were clustered apart, talking volubly among themselves.

The sherbet vendors were plying a wonderful trade.

This was Damascus – one of the pearls of the Orient – and its citizens were enjoying themselves.

I, as a visitor, imagined that it was a public holiday, but it was soon evident that this was an occasion which even transcended such mass amusement.

Syria was not a country united by race, religion or customs and its inhabitants, many of them mutually antagonistic, had only one point of cohesion: the demonstration.

Agitation gives an opportunity for enjoyment which cannot be compared with anything attaching to the many public holidays. Agitation means temporary turmoil under the cover of which much can be accomplished.

College students, scenting the possibility of a long strike, take sides indiscriminately. After all, they have to enjoy themselves while they are young. The women, with the adaptability of their sex, welcome the excitement. When the attentions of their menfolk are diverted there is much that can be done which is dear to the feminine mind. As for the men; well, any occasion which tends to distract from the grind of daily toil is more than welcome and it does them good to exercise their vocal organs.

We should not forget that, since the early twentieth century, street demonstrations in the Middle East have usually had their roots in a promise made to the people and then disowned. It might have been the Ottomans, the Western Powers, or someone else: but how would we feel and act in their place?

The very first time I was in Syria, the French, though utterly confused in mind, were trying to rule the country. They had been awarded a Mandate by the League of Nations, and went about their task in a bizarrely logical manner which sat but uneasily upon their fiery Latin temperament. Demonstrations were at their height. Many were about nothing at all, according to the French officials, high and low, whom I contacted. This was true – if you forgot the suppressed passions of a people administered by foreigners.

'Down with the Mandate,' yelled the students, and the police discreetly effaced themselves. Wistfully they gazed upon the demonstrations from a distance. It would be amusing to join in the fun but, after all, they had to be careful. The assembly was more or less orderly, and a little honest shouting did no-one any harm. Besides, it was embarrassing to be called upon to arrest, say, one's cousin or brother-in-law. It was inconvenient at home where the womenfolk failed to understand the workings of government, and the neighbours were inclined to be supercilious.

It was upon a scene much like this that I gazed as I made my way into Damascus.

Soon the demonstrators were joined by others.

Hurriedly, shops were closed, and the shopkeepers hastened to join in the revels. The crowd outside the Government Offices was now large.

'What is the demonstration about?' I asked one man, who was howling like a jackal.

He looked at me blankly, shrugged his shoulders and howled the louder.

Turning to another demonstrator, I once again sought enlightenment.

'Oh,' he said in response to my query, 'a priest has been arrested and it is a religious matter.'

'It was not a priest,' interjected the jackal, pausing momentarily in his howling. 'It is said that a request by the Alouites has wrongly been turned down by the High Commissioner.'

'Nothing of the sort,' vehemently protested his neighbour. 'This demonstration is to force upon the authorities our sense of displeasure regarding the new tax scale.'

'Down with the tyrants,' bawled the students and venom and point was added to their demonstration as they thought of the professors waiting in the colleges ready, on the return of the young men, further to torment the youth of the nation with unnecessary equations in a variety of unknowns.

'Tell these idiots from Paris that the Crusades are now over!' roared a Bedouin with a very dangerous-looking rifle.

And all in a temperature of 105 degrees Fahrenheit, in the shade.

After a while there was a seething commotion amongst those nearest the entrance to the offices; soon it went through the crowd that there was no point to the demonstration. It had all been a mistake. No priest had been arrested, nobody had taken umbrage. What had happened was that a long-wanted robber had been brought in from the hills.

Reluctantly, the crowd began to disperse.

Dejectedly, the students thought of the problems which still remained to be worked out. The men returned slowly and disconsolately to their labours. Shops were reopened – and the women decorously drooped their eyelids once more.

In the Government Offices, the typewriters clicked again and here, as well as without, Damascus returned to its sleepy, restful, Oriental rhythm.

Unfortunately, no picture of Damascus would be complete without an early reference to the turbulent spirit of the Syrian. This seems to be part of the national character. Perhaps it is unfair and, in a sense untrue, so to refer to this trait. It would be more exact to say that it has always been there, but it is only since 1918 that an outlet has been found for it.

My province does not include the sphere of international politics, and it was my intention, when I started to record these pages, vigorously and steadfastly to steer clear of the subject.

Yet, at this stage it obtrudes. Politics appears because it must – even if my incursion is but a brief and a cursory one.

It had been the custom in many quarters, not least among the local people, largely to blame the French for the dissatisfaction of the Syrian and the fragmentation of the Lebanon. The word 'maladministration' was one that had been worked almost to death. Yet these critics were not entirely fair.

The trouble, such as it was, could be traced back to the days immediately after the cessation of World War I.

In November, 1918, Great Britain joined with France in

the issue of a manifesto which fired the blood of the Druses and the Syrian Arabs alike. The people of Syria were told that:

> 'The end that France and Great Britain have in pursuing, in the East, the War unloosed by German ambition, is the complete and definite freeing of the peoples so long oppressed by the Turks, and the establishment of national Governments and Administrations deriving their authority from the initiative and free choice of the indigenous populations.
>
> 'In order to give effect to these intentions, France and Great Britain have agreed to encourage and assist the establishment of indigenous Governments and Administrations in Syria and Mesopotamia, now freed by the Allies, and in the territories whose liberation they seek, and to recognise them as soon as they are effectively established.'

The peoples of Syria, looking to the progress which had been made under Mandatory administrations in Palestine, Iraq and elsewhere, were soon impatient for these promises to be honoured. Possessed of a large and valuable agricultural sector, endowed with an intelligent and relatively well-educated populace, they felt that they deserved more than the status, virtually, of a colony.

It is not for me to say that it was unfortunate for the Syrians that France should have been selected as the mandatory Power. One can only refer to the established fact that France is traditionally unpopular both with the majority of the Arabs and with the Druse. This attitude partly had its genesis in the events of 1860, when a French expedition went to Damascus following a massacre of Christians.

The Syrians have been apt to look upon the French as conquerors and the problems of the French administration were, therefore, all the more complex.

The man who had been the target of most of the blame was General Sarrail. His name was held in execration by the Syrians and especially by the Druses upon whom fell the weight of his vengeance after a series of unhappy revolts. But the Syrian is apt to forget that his struggle for early emancipation was made the more difficult by its very violence. The French saw a people composed of many races and creeds enmeshed in the coils of internecine antagonism and they themselves at a great disadvantage.

They early, and very rightly, adopted the principle of abstaining from any action which would cause offence to the religious susceptibilities of the many different sects – a principle which all European Governments accepted, just as Napoleon and Augustus had done earlier.

Yet how troublesome this principle can be! Half the disputes which arose throughout the land of Syria had a religious significance and the official who would abide by the commanding principle to the letter must indeed have an agile mind.

It was said that such a man, in fact, had not yet been born. Certain it was that something in the mental set of many Westerners made it difficult to understand the East.

One official said to me during the course of my early wanderings: 'You are an Oriental, and so perhaps you can explain this to me. A man came to my office, supplicating, it does not matter for what. He approached me with the greatest deference and poured praises upon my head. He recited from the literature of the Sufis and addressing me said:

"The sun will drink you up,
You will become that rosy cloud
Which will dissolve in rain upon the land of Men
And of bright roses
Which you will fertilise.
Then when winter
Turns you into snow
The Spring sunshine will drink you up . . ."

'I wrote it down at the time, since it seemed interesting . . .'

I could hardly forbear to smile. The idea of this bucolic, large-framed, lumbering Frenchman (although he spoke Arabic perfectly) becoming a cloud to scatter sweetness upon the land was a ludicrous one; even allowing for the allegory of the poetical mind and the supplicant. He went on:

'Yes, here I was to be the fertiliser of roses and all because this man wanted me to do his enemy an ill turn. When I refused, as, of course, I had to do, he made his way out of my office, salaaming and calling down the blessings of Allah upon me against the time when I should change my mind.

'A few minutes after the man's departure I also had to leave. On the doorstep I was surprised to see that my visitor still lingered. He was busily engaged in spitting upon an inoffensive stone. Meanwhile he was calling me 'Shaitan, and Afrit' – Satan and demon – and any other term of denunciation which came into his head.'

It is this fundamental difference in outlook between the French and the Syrians which did not help the development of the people – even in things which the West could learn from the East!

Approaching Damascus from the heights above Sala-hiyeh, one looks down upon groves of cypress and olive trees. Between them there are groves of lemon and other fruit trees, all giving to the sunlit landscape their own shade of kaleidoscopic colour. This strikingly magnificent panorama extends for miles. From among the colours of the blossoms, one discerns the shapes of roofs and domes of palaces and mosques.

The scene, for the weary traveller, is serene and up-lifting. One realises that this is a stage on which have been enacted great historical events. It was here, in a street which was once 'called Straight' that Saul of Tarsus lodged in the House of Judas. It was here, in the first flush of the triumph of Islam, that the Arabs held sway, extending their rule to the Atlantic on the one hand, and to the banks of the River Oxus in Central Asia on the other. Once Damascus was the capital of the Arabs' vast dominions. Even now it is fascinating and reflects much of its past glories; much of its past power and riches.

An addition to the Arabian Nights' atmosphere is made by the many sparkling streams which flow from the hills through the fruit gardens; by the fact that the majority of the buildings are white and dazzling in the rays of the sun; and by the fact that the East is the East and notwith-standing modernism of all kinds, it is really unchanging in its essence.

Quite apart from the mosques and palaces which are in themselves sufficient to give Damascus an Oriental air of opulence and theological austerity, there are the miles of wonderful bazaars to which the most precious of the wares of Asia have been attracted throughout the centuries.

Here are to be found antiquities of all kinds: real and spurious, of course. Rare swords and scimitars with glori-ous blades of tempered steel, magnificent gems, luxurious silks, costly carpets – all displayed at stalls by grey-bearded Arab vendors. And the bargaining! This is an art in itself, requiring patience and an insight into Oriental psychology. Because this is so frequently lacking, European tourists often pay fantastic prices for the wares of Damascus or go away disappointed.

No self-respecting vendor in a Damascus souk would dream of asking less than three times the price he would be prepared to accept. Haggling is all part of his creed. It is inherent in the situation; an essential salve to his conscience.

He has to pretend to himself that he does not really desire to dispose of his wares and that in finally selling, he is doing so more for the welfare of the purchaser than for his own.

There is something just a tiny bit *infra dig* in trade in the mind of many a Moslem and in descending to deal with his customer there are finer, inner points of conscience that have to be placated.

It takes a whole morning, with perhaps a final session in the afternoon, to purchase a valuable rug with true ceremony and decorum.

One must sit in the shade of the stall, drink sherbet or Turkish coffee and even smoke Turkish cigarettes. Now and again one makes a passing reference to carpets, but never really *talks* about them. Because there are carpets around one, it is in keeping that one should, out of mere politeness, make an occasional point on colours and stitches, but this is to keep the conversation together and not because one is constrained to buy.

The American and the Englishman descend upon the bazaars of Damascus, march resolutely up to a carpet-vendor and ask to see his stock.

With a hurt expression, the merchant proceeds to

display his wares, but that cord of sympathy between vendor and purchaser has been snapped before it has been established.

Neither the American nor the Englishman will feel happy lolling languorously upon cushions seductively placed in the shade. They parade steadfastly up and down with the exhausting, nervous, mechanical efficiency of their kind and the next words they utter are:

'How much?'

Where is the symmetry and poetry of language; that which is essentially part of the poem in silk or wool which the Westerner wishes to buy?

'So much,' says the Arab, diffidently, knowing full well that he would accept a quarter of the price.

'Too much,' says the Englishman and the American artfully, for they have read their guide-books well. 'We will give you half.'

If the vendor has no sons whose wedding is at hand, or if he has succeeded in pulling some of his carpet wool over the eyes of the tax collector, he will probably draw on his dignity and proceed to explain how to accept such a price would entail the ruination of himself and his family, for the next few generations.

Before he has half finished, the Englishman and the American are at the next-door stall.

Should he really be in urgent need of money he will demur, yet accept the offer of half, finding solace in the reflection that all Westerners are fools, anyway.

As an Oriental, I will give a tip to Western visitors to the bazaars of Damascus, and many another part of the East.

If possible, always time your advent for Friday morning. The Arab vendor believes that if he makes an early sale on Friday, his luck will be good for the ensuing week. He will not want his first potential customer to leave without a purchase. He will size you up and mentally count the contents of your wallet, but he will not pitch his price too high.

He will not, of course, rob himself, but if you display signs of going elsewhere, he will not rob you.

No-one should visit Damascus without seeing the souks of the silversmiths, the coppersmiths and the other metal-workers. These bazaars are features of the life of other great Oriental cities, but the workers of Damascus have an inherent skill and artistry which makes their products famous the world over. In these bazaars are to be found ornaments of the most delicate workmanship – work which is finer than that executed by the craftsmen of Istanbul or Delhi.

Then there will be found a profusion of amber and turquoise amulets. These serve to adorn the hair of the children and also of the Arab horse, for they are said to possess the property of warding off evil spirits and the effects of the evil eye. Amusing too, in its way, is the old Clothes Bazaar – but only when one wants a reaction from the sublime to the ridiculous.

All Christians, very naturally, ask to be directed to 'The Street which is called Straight'. Doubtless during the time of Judas and Saul it was worthy of its name. Then, it was typically straight and Roman in character, its sides being adorned with pillars. Now its outline is irregular, shops and other buildings having been built with a true Eastern disregard for the Western cult of symmetry as exemplified by the dignity of simplicity and the ruler.

It is among the mosques of Damascus that the Christian of the Western world discovers how closely the Moslem faith is allied to his own. Many Westerners express their astonishment that this should be so, mainly because, I suppose, their history books only have regard for the wars between the Cross and the Crescent. Many Westerners visit the mosques of Damascus and leave with a sense of unreality and bewilderment.

The greatest mosque of all – the Umayyad – is in itself a magnificent structure. It vies in splendour with the Dome of the Rock at Jerusalem and it is almost as highly venerated by the Moslem, though less in rank than the mosques of Mecca and Medina. Unfortunately, this El Umawi is encumbered by small dwellings and no true conception of its beauty and its greatness can be obtained without considerable trouble.

The site of El Umawi was hallowed long before the days of the Prophet. A Greek temple once stood on the spot and later, when Constantine was converted to Christianity, a church in the form of a basilica was erected there.

This church now forms the centre of the mosque – this being, of course, only one of those examples where Christian churches were transformed into Moslem places of worship. Lest it be thought that such conversions are unusual, it could be added that there seem to be as many instances where mosques have been transformed into Christian churches. There is one notable instance in Lahore, the capital of the Punjab, where a great Moslem mosque was long used as the parish church by the European community. Later, when a cathedral was built, the mosque was transformed yet again, but this time into a government library! And, of course, hundreds or perhaps thousands of mosques in Arab Spain were on the sites of present-day churches.

One of the tombs of El Umawi is said to contain the head of John the Baptist. This shrine is held in great veneration by Moslems all over the world. Until the Young Turks secured control of Constantinople, it was the custom for each successive Ottoman Sultan to send to the shrine a sacred covering on the occasion of his coronation.

The graceful minarets of this mosque will catch the eye of the visitor. Westerners, especially, should ask to have pointed out to them one in particular. It is conspicuous because it has a crescent on its long, tapering summit.

The name applied to this minaret is the Minarat Isa – in other words, the Minaret of Christ. Some believe that Jesus will descend upon this minaret on the day of Judgment.

Not so many yards away is the tomb of the great Saladin, the amazingly successful Saracen hero of seven centuries ago. His tomb is to be found in a pleasant garden. The mausoleum contains the sarcophagus of the famous conqueror. Originally the sarcophagus was encased in painted woodwork which at least harmonised with its surroundings. Now unfortunately, like so many other places in the Near East, it bears the inartistic handiwork of the German ex-Kaiser. During his sensational tour of Palestine and Syria, when so much vandalism was allowed in order to pander to his extraordinary vanity, he caused the wooden covering of the sarcophagus to be removed. In its place were erected marble slabs in the German national colours!

True, the Emperor did place his sword at the feet of the Kurdish emperor. But that was not all. Above the sarcophagus is a priceless antique chandelier. On this are panels upon which 'S.S', Sultan Saladin's initials, were inscribed. The boorish German potentate had the lettering obliterated on every alternate panel and the monogram 'W.W' substituted. Perhaps he will go down in history as 'Wacky Wilhelm'. He deserves little less.

The old walls of the city are well worth a visit, if only because of their impressiveness. The walls are built of large blocks of stone faintly reminiscent of the pyramids of Giza. They are so heavy that they hold together without the aid of cement or mortar.

The Babkisan gateway has been closed for several hundred years, but alongside of it are the ruins of St. Paul's tower. It was from here that the Apostle was lowered in a basket.

The palaces of the wealthy Arabs are rather difficult to inspect at close quarters, but if one were sufficiently fortunate to obtain entry, the visitor would be amazed by the luxury to be found in these homes of the rich.

The exteriors invariably have an atmosphere of forbidding gloom, but once beyond the giant gates there is a fairyland of fountains, courts and gardens, beautiful trees, aromatic shrubs and a wonderful variety of flowers.

The courts are covered with mosaic paving and the verandas screened by magnificently chiselled marble of dazzling whiteness. Some of the ancient mosaics, dating back to Classical times, are far more impressive than many which one sees displayed in the West as unexcelled miracles of workmanship.

At one time, visitors could at least inspect the Palace of Azm. True, it had been converted into a museum, but it retained much of that charm which it possessed when it was a private residence. Now it is but a heap of stone, forlorn in the midst of other ruins. When the French found it necessary to bombard Damascus, the Palace of Azm seemed to exercise a fascination upon the gunners of the Mandate. In any event, they gave it their complete attention until, with many surrounding buildings of note, it was razed to the ground.

One could spend many moons amid the fascination and

the intrigues of Damascus, but a traveller is a traveller and
he has to get on.

From Damascus, I had intended to make my way
through the hills of Lebanon to Beirut and from thence to
the incredibly ancient city of Baalbek. It is some sixty
miles from Damascus to Beirut and I found the road to be
a remarkably good one.

I had been quite prepared to make the journey by
camel, but in the course of my wanderings in that great
Damascus souk, the Hamidiyya, I came across a cheery
rogue named Yakub who was the proud possessor of a
battered truck. Yakub had to take this juggernaut to
Beirut and for a slight consideration, he offered to take me
with him.

Yakub was a remarkable talker and, I suspected, a great
thief. We spent two nights on the road to Beirut, while
Yakub waited and bargained regarding the transport of
merchandise, and each evening we dined on chicken. I am
reasonably certain that Yakub did not pay for these delicacies but I have to add humbly that my suspicions in this
regard in no way detracted from the flavour of our repasts.

Yakub, as I have said, was garrulous and, moreover, he
could make himself heard above the roar and rattle of his
ancient engine which, obviously enough, was a relic of the
First War. However, in a sense, it seemed to fit in with its
historical surroundings better than something modern
would have done.

I have to record, nevertheless, a somewhat painful incident when a long train of some two hundred camels,
which we overtook some eighteen kilometres out of Damascus, regarded his equipage with evident disgust.

We had hooted and ground our way past two-thirds of
the snorting, snarling procession, amidst the by no means
polite remarks of the half dozen Arab attendants, when

the leaders took fright and, with wild lunges of their ungainly legs, they went scampering pell-mell for Beirut.

The hundred odd animals which we had passed then took up the challenge to ancient modernity and speedily went by us in dense clouds of dust.

In a cloud of his own, entirely of profanity, Yakub induced his Ford to cease from labour until the lumbering, unwieldy menagerie had outdistanced us by some hundred yards. Then, with his eye agleam with mischief, he started up again. Such were the discordant, indecent noises he produced from this product of Detroit that he scared those camels over a distance of many miles – all the way, indeed, to the caravanserai where we were to stop the night.

What the camelmen said to Yakub and me when they had finally calmed their frightened charges is not for inclusion here. I recall, however, that their leader, a venerable Arab, palsied with anger, did not cease in his anathematising until he had scandalised us and our relatives for many generations past.

And for once Yakub was phlegmatic.

'Camels,' he muttered. 'I never did like the brutes. We had to eat them during the War!'

Yakub was a very amusing personage with a strange philosophy of his own. In his way, he was a busy man and that perhaps explained his contempt for politics and anything beyond the orbit of his own particular place in life.

He did not mourn the passing of the Turks, but the only use he had for the French lay in the fact that they built roads upon which one could run an ancient and dilapidated Ford.

As for legislative councils, parliaments, civil courts and all those extraordinarily cumbersome pieces of legislative

or executive machinery which go with the Western political complex, he had a supreme contempt for them all.

He was an opportunist in his small way. He frankly
lamented the cessation of the War because then, as he
naively put it, one could ask any price for eggs and other
farm produce and be certain of receiving it. His lorry
marked the culmination of a successful period of war
profiteering.

I really am quite unable to apportion my indebtedness
between Yakub and Mr. Henry Ford. Yakub displayed an
astonishing dexterity in the manipulation of string-tied
controls and a fatalistic confidence in the groundwork of
Mr. Ford as we panted up or thundered down those hilly
roads.

He assured me that he travelled quickly down one
incline so that the momentum would assist him in mounting the next. Never once, however, did he put his foot on
the brake-pedal. It would have been a waste of energy. His
brake drums had burnt out long ago.

During the intervals when I was not hanging grimly on
to that decrepit lorry and wondering where Yakub's supreme optimism would eventually land us, I was able to
observe the hills covered with olive trees and the great
variety of flowering shrubs. Through these it was possible
to discern glimpses of the mountains of Lebanon. And the
hills were in varying shades of green – placid and restful
for the traveller and in striking contrast to those with
which one meets in the arid countries to the south.

It was with a certain measure of relief that I placed my
feet upon the streets of the port of Beirut and bade farewell
to Yakub. At heart, I am certain, he is a nomad. A few
years ago he would have despised any means of mechanical
locomotion and would have been content with a Bedouin's

tent. But, after all, a truck carries more than a camel can: and if there are roads . . .

And the rascal had been through my knapsack before we parted. My only consolation was that he found but little.

Beirut – once a great Levantine port – was now a disappointing seaport town from which most of the ancient glory has faded. Yes, 'faded' is an excellent term. One felt that there was much here that should interest the antiquarian, and then discovered that it was merely an excellent place from which to commence a tour – and as quickly as possible.

Perhaps, however, Yakub's lorry had upset my liver. In any case, I left rapidly for Baalbek.

I made Baalbek by road and my means of transport this time was an ass, every bit as hard and as knobbly as Yakub's Ford. Our road took us to a height of 3,500 feet and, long before we could see the modern Baalbek, there were the ancient ruins clearly visible – the great walls of the Acropolis – the marble columns – the vast courts and temples – the relics of a past and forgotten age.

In other places which have been deserted, one is conscious of a certain air of romantic mystery. One senses this when visiting the several past cities of Delhi or when wandering around the perfectly preserved palaces of Fatehpur Sikri. But in Baalbek there is something else which assails one – a dim impression that one is probing beyond the ordinary confines of human intelligence; that one is on a spot where the brain refuses adequately to react to the true measure of the passing of time.

There is something tremendously tangible about the pyramids. One can gaze upon the Sphinx and the passage of the years becomes relative, but in Baalbek, one's impressions are only fleeting. Nevertheless, they are impressively vivid; as if something has happened here: but what? Quite an uncanny feeling . . .

Baalbek is unquestionably one of the very, very old sites of the East. Around it, legend has woven many fancies. Tradition has handed down many a fantastic story.

Cain is said to have been its founder.

Nimrod it was, who built a great tower rising to the skies.

It was here that Solomon raised his temple to Baal.

Baalbek, on the road which led from the East to Tyre, was very much on the map in early biblical times.

There are, however, no traces of Nimrod's tower and none of Solomon's temple to Baal – at least none is at present visible though it may be that the excavators of the future will unearth some interesting finds.

On these very ancient archaeological fields, successive civilisations have eradicated evidence of those which went before. Thus we find that, at Baalbek, Baal was afterwards associated with Helios, the Sun God, during the Greek occupation. Baalbek was then called Heliopolis.

When, in the first century A.D., the Romans held sway over this site, they added to the rapidly declining worship of Baal that of Jupiter, Venus and Mercury. Consequently, the ruins we see today are of Greek and Roman origin.

On a raised platform, facing the entrance to the Acropolis, and commanding the surrounding country, is all that remains of the Temple of the Sun and Jupiter. Although only the outer columns remain standing, it is possible to visualise from these much of the ancient glory and grandeur of this ancient centre of worship.

With its façade and doorway still clearly decorated with garlands of wheat, flowers and grapes as offerings to Bacchus, is the Temple to the god of that name. This, too, is in the shadow of the Acropolis. Of the original forty-six monolithic columns, nearly twenty remain upright and they contrive to hold up the immense, richly carved marble blocks which form the entablature and supports of the roof.

The Temple of Bacchus is quite well-preserved and it is one of the most striking and most beautiful in the country. It combines in its bold architectural outline a remarkable delicacy of sculpture.

Vying in grandeur with the ruins of Baalbek, are those of the amazing desert city of Zenobia – a site which still commemorates the name of one of the most remarkable women in history.

Queen Zenobia flourished in the third century and she carved for herself a mighty empire extending from Persia to Egypt. This great Queen was of mixed Arab, Greek and Egyptian descent and she seems to have exercised a powerful psychological influence over her peoples.

Always could she inspire them to great deeds and to conquest after conquest. However, ambition and jealousy proved to be her greatest enemies. She was foolish enough to pit her strength against the Roman Emperor Aurelian.

Many fierce battles were waged in the vicinity of Homs and Hama, in which the redoubtable Zenobia was always to be found at the head of her troops. However, her mystic powers proved of small avail against the mighty Roman war machine and she was eventually made captive and led away to Rome.

The historian Gibbon tells us that she ended her days as a comfortable Roman matron, but he was sometimes inclined to be sentimental. Other writers, and particularly Zosimus, maintain that Zenobia was truculent to the last. According to these sources, she scorned the advances of her Roman conquerors, refused food, and speedily died.

The City of Zenobia, however, is quite a far cry from Beirut.

I decided to spend some days among the Bedouins who congregate in this area. I had been fortunate enough to make the acquaintance of a rich sheep-owner who contemplated a tour of the encampments. Attaching myself to his camel cavalcade, I spent several carefree days enjoying the hospitality of the Bedouin. The nomad tent-dwellers still camp around the Arab town of Homs as they did thousands of years ago. Homs is mentioned by Pliny as the birthplace of one of the high priests of Baal who became a Roman Emperor, but little of its former greatness remains. Lofty minarets still stand and the mosque of Sidi Khaled still possesses some priceless old carpets; but there is little else.

Frequently in our journeys between Homs and Palmyra (as Zenobia's city is now named), we crossed the old Roman road. Parts of the original paving are still to be seen and, here and there, one comes across an old Roman milestone still doing duty.

It is in this area that the desert opens out toward Baghdad and a deep-rooted weed covers the sandy waste in many parts. This weed, a sickly green in the spring, but a withered, unappetising thing in the heat of the summer, is what has attracted the Bedouin shepherds through the centuries.

An ordinary observer would state that no animal could exist on such fodder, but the nomads' sheep are as wily and resourceful as those who tend them. They have an astonishing quality of stamina and they can find food and nourishment where less hardy specimens would die. When all else fails them, these sheep nibble away the sand from the roots of this weed and upon these roots they succeed in living until the winter months: when rain comes to revitalise the desert.

Most of the tent-dwellers are exceedingly poor. The shepherd receives no money for his work, but only a certain number of lambs provided that the sheep are returned to the owner in good condition. Yet the Bedouin is a cheerful mortal.

It is always advisable, by the way, to approach these habitations with extreme caution. This is not because, as the scenario writers would have it, of the danger of being fired upon by the Bedouin, but because of the attentions of hideously savage dogs of which every tent seems to have an uncomfortably large complement. These animals will rush forth like a pack of wolves and go leaping and snarling around intruders, and there are no trees to shin up in the desert! They only consent to be quietened by someone they know.

The Bedouin tents would hardly suit the fastidious tastes of those young damsels who may be struck by the glamour and romance of Sheikhdom. They are spacious enough affairs, but in them the Bedouin accommodates everything that is his – his pots and his pans, his receptacles for storing butter and cheese, his clothing, his rugs, his chickens, his dogs, his innumerable children and his women.

The Arab women are never idle. When they are not attending to their children or inducing the poultry to behave with a due sense of decorum before visitors, they sit in the background making butter. These women pour sheep's milk into a large skin suspended from the roof of the tent. This skin they rock to and fro, singing mournful Arab songs the while with a dirgelike rhythm.

They continue the churning, both of butter and of their dirges, for hours on end.

It was in this way that butter was made thousands of years ago, and the Bedouin's habits are unchanging.

What would be more simple than to attach small skins to the very animals that provide the milk? As they graze and grub at the weeds of the desert they would provide sufficient movement to the milk to turn it into butter.

Such a simple innovation, however, which only occurred to me as an incidental thought, would be too revolutionary for the nomadic mind. It is one thing to tackle what Fate may throw at you. To tempt Fate by changing things which do not cry out for change is another matter altogether. With the American of the fable, the nomad seems to think, 'if it ain't broke, don't fix it'.

Palmyra, Zenobia's city, is now but an oasis in the desert. There are groves of palm and fruit trees and tiny rivulets winding among them, giving to the oasis a green hue in refreshing contrast to the muddy yellow of the sands of the surrounding desert.

In its heyday, there were aqueducts of massive stone built over high arches to conduct the water from springs in the hills some five or six miles away, but these have mostly disappeared. Near one of the outer walls, one yet remains to remind us of the greatness of the Queen.

Palmyra was once known as Tadmor and it was then the great granary of Solomon. Situated on the great trade-route from the Euphrates to Egypt, it was a meeting-place between the East and the West.

Doubtless its waters were what first caused people to pause and settle at this spot. To this day, a hot sulphur spring called Ephca flows here, celebrated for its curative powers. The waters issue from a subterranean grotto. If one can withstand the pungent smell (and taste), it is possible to swim into this grotto for several hundred yards.

Palmyra is a city which has undergone many vicissitudes. Mark Antony captured it and despoiled it and Hadrian ruled there in the second century. Above them all, however, will always stand the name of Zenobia.

In Palmyra there is a great Temple of the Sun which is, unfortunately, now encumbered with many Arab dwellings. The ruin covers an area of several thousand square yards, yet even as it is, it is most impressive. It is easy to judge also of its magnificence in the days of its early glories. Columns seventy feet high, in rows, adorned the outer court. There were several hundred of these and many of them still remain erect. From the outer court, steps led up to the middle temple. The entrancingly carved ceiling of this is still there as an evidence of the love of craftsmanship of the ancients.

From the avenues of marble columns which lead through the Triumphal Arch, one sees the Necropolis more than a mile away on the lower slopes of the hills.

Some of the tombs in the Necropolis, built of red sandstone, are more than one hundred feet high. Their many storeys tower into the air and there are some with receptacles enough to hold from four to five hundred bodies. None of these now contains any visible human remains.

I climbed laboriously up the stone steps of one of these tombs and from the summit had a wonderful view of Palmyra and the surrounding desert. Inscriptions on some of the tombs date from the first century.

I would have liked to have stayed longer in Palmyra, but the Arab sheep-owner from Beirut was anxious to be on the move once more.

We watered our camels at one of the rivulets and then commenced a steady, monotonous journey to Homs where I bade farewell to this very excellent friend.

Perhaps I should digress here to remark on the Syrian

trotting camel. The best animals have quite lengthy coats which are carefully groomed. Soft and silky to the touch, the hair is of a light yellow colour.

Extraordinary stories are told about the length of time that camels can exist without water. Some who subscribe to the fantastic readily believe that one drink will suffice a camel for three weeks. In point of fact, to keep a Syrian trotting camel in proper condition, it should be watered at regular intervals of three days.

Out in the desert, of course this is not always possible and sometimes the camels have to pass a waterless period of six or seven days. When this occurs, however, they speedily become jaded. They continually regurgitate that rather revolting bag which, with a shuddering gurgle, they can protrude from their mouths, and display other signs of distress.

And the actual watering of a camel is an art in itself.

Led to a trough or a stream it will superciliously and disdainfully contemplate the water for some minutes. Then it will consent to lower its head and to drink for a moment or two. Then its head will rise again and it will stare stupidly around, perhaps for ten minutes at a time.

One unaccustomed to the way of camels would conclude that the animal had drunk its fill, but that is not so.

Fortunately, time is of no great moment in the desert, for just when a city man would be losing patience, the camel drops his head again and has another short drink.

This process goes on for an hour or more.

The Bedouins have sufficient sense never to harry or hurry their animals at the watering places for they can never be certain when they will reach the next oasis. An indifferently watered camel is likely to flounder on a long desert trek and to leave its rider marooned.

Those long sprawling legs of the camel are ideal for

negotiating the desert sands, but frequently the caravans have to take to the hills where they slide and slither down rocky inclines and pick a tortuous way through boulder-strewn ravines.

A loaded camel on a rocky hillside is a pitiable object. As he places his great, pad-like feet on stones that slide beneath them he squeals in evident terror.

And he has reason to be apprehensive. When a camel goes down in such conditions his legs invariably 'star' about him, ripping open his under portion and making immediate meat for the vultures and the jackals.

These Syrian trotting camels have a surprising turn of speed – and they can gallop with zest and at an alarming rate – alarming, that is, if one is perched precariously above.

In many parts of the East the camel is ridden astride, and with stirrups. In Syria and Palestine one perches on a tiny seat in the region of the hump and then crosses the ankles, left foot over the right, on the animal's shoulders.

The long, curved neck looms up and reaches into the distance from between one's heels. Away on the horizon is the camel's nose and through the nostrils passes a string. The other end of this is held in the hand and one has to remember to keep it loose.

If, in the tribulations of trotting or galloping, one happens to pull the string taut, the camel loses speed, stops, follows the drag on its nostrils, curls that elastic neck, stares one unpleasantly in the face, snarls, grinds its green, foamy, saliva-laden teeth – and regurgitates.

To make a Syrian camel gallop, one kicks him on the left shoulder with the heel of one's boot. To stop him, one negotiates the string and hopes for the best.

Envoi:
The Reason for my Travels

Now travelling is travelling, and mystical quests are something else. I made the journeys from which are taken the highlights in this book, both for enjoyment and to carry out missions connected with the Sufis.

Have you noticed that people who belong to cults and religions, systems and programmes, constantly foist them upon you? That, or else they are being mysterious about them.

Point one: the Sufis are not a cult, so:–

> This book is composed of tales and experiences which I have found most acceptable when told on the radio, or during story-telling sessions (in caravanserais or elsewhere) – or even simply after dinner: admittedly sometimes in exotic places and strange company.

And, you will have noticed, I have not said much about the Sufis in it. If you are not at all interested in them or their way of life, now is your chance to stop reading this book; for it contains, after this, very little about my travels.

If you would like to be put on our mailing list and to receive our catalogue please fill in and return this card.

Name ....

Address ....

....

Country & Postcode ....

Envoi: The Reason for my Travels

I was delighted to have had your company and – goodbye.

Others may note that almost anything which they may have read (especially in learned books) about the Sufis is very inaccurate. In the West especially, people have tried to portray Sufis by analogy with Western monks: they are wrong. They have also been at pains to trace Sufi history: and they have got it – you are right – wrong. They have amalgamated bits and pieces of Sufi ideas and observance into their own religious and other systems: this is an activity which is totally wrong if results are to be expected.

In contemporary terms, the Sufis can be seen as people who, initially, work against the evils of coercive organised religion and restrictive cults; then try to help expand the understanding of those who are interested: strictly according to the potential of the people and the times.

This latter contention is in itself almost unbelievable and unexpected. Certainly it is unacceptable to the vast majority of people, who cannot feel happy with it at all. Why? Simply because they always need the reassurance of tradition and of the familiar. If they don't know what to reject, they may deify it.

If the Sufi is teaching by means of modern concepts, the traditionalists are appalled. The modern-minded ones, by contrast, will recoil from what are to them old-fashioned ideas. In Sufic terms, such people do not really exist as far as their potential for development is concerned.

I made my journeys at the behest of the Sufis, in order to bring some of these conceptions to individuals and to communities throughout the Middle Eastern countries visited.

Some were interested, some were excited. Mostly, they were appalled.

Perhaps it was I who benefited most.

You can probably imagine the consternation, even the utter dislike, on the part of groups of friends, companions, earnest seekers of the truth, when told that the groups' composition was useless because, according to Sufi experience, self-collected learning classes could not harmonise.

And, of course, there was a vicious circle situation when they demanded to be shown what that precise experience was...

Most associations of people, of course, have their own power structure, with some in authority, and some gaining their satisfactions by being controlled or influenced by those in authority. Just picture such a grouping (and which are not like this?) when a beardless youth, albeit with the very best credentials, appears in their midst, contradicting what they accept as the very cement of their organisation!

And there is more. People will not remove obstacles in their path, even when these obstacles are the precise things which impede their progress.

Can you imagine telling almost anyone that excitement, physical activity of certain accepted kinds, some music even, run counter to their best interests?

Or that self-selected study is useless, since it is like asking a drug addict to nominate his own poison.

Or that 'idolatry', 'intoxication' and 'addiction' can exist in the most supposedly holy or materialistic people, more powerfully than if they had a clay idol, a bottle of spirits or a hypodermic of heroin?

'The spiritual practices which we have are only preparatory; are diluted, are mistaken, confused, counter-productive? Get to hell out of here!' That is the message I was often invited to take back to my principals; even when we were only responding to a cry for help.

Above all, the bugbear of the Sufis is not, as one might imagine, to struggle against materialism. It is to handle two very powerful distortions in the customary thinking of people everywhere.

The first of these is to accumulate ideas, especially from the East, in the belief that these must be of some value, when many of the most popular ones frankly originate from fraudulent or now-irrelevant, inoperative sources, however ancient. The second is to imagine that, because there is no such thing, for the most part, in mystico-religion or philosophy in the West, an understanding beyond normal human knowledge cannot exist.

It is this last-named barrier which proved, and still proves, most difficult. People, even the most erudite, the most renowned, the most important (as well as simple people) would constantly exclaim to me about this.

They said, as if it were proof: 'If the Sufis know all these things, why do they communicate through people like you, who do not even know the superficialities, as you call them, of religion and metaphysics?'

Deliberately or otherwise, of course, such a remark ignores the fact that, if the first allegation is true, it explains everything. That is, if the Sufis can see further, they can see that this is the only way to break through. Further, if that which is called spiritual elsewhere, is only emotional excitement, the Sufis cannot use this to communicate with, since it does not carry information, let alone enlightenment.

And all of this is not to mention the vast stock of 'ideas' which are buffering ones: put into circulation, over the centuries, by Sufis in order to prevent 'psychic burglars' from causing trouble . . .

215